Ask Me Sr

LANGUAGE ARTS

SOCIAL STUDIES

SCIENCE

MATH

Grade 4

Comprehensive, Curriculum-aligned Questions and Answers for
4th Grade

By Donna M. Roszak

Part of the **Ask Me Smarter!** Series
Empowering parents to empower their kids with essential knowledge!

Ask Me Smarter!

LANGUAGE ARTS, SOCIAL STUDIES, SCIENCE, and MATH - GRADE 4

Comprehensive, Curriculum-aligned Questions and Answers for 4th Grade

Empowering parents to empower their kids with essential knowledge.
AMS! - Making knowledge **FUN**-da-men-tal!

Published in the United States by: Zebra Print Press, LLC
Cedarburg, WI U.S.A.

Cover Design by Donna M. Roszak

Library of Congress Control Number: 2020906857

ISBN: 978-0-9860801-8-0

Library of Congress Control Number: 2020906857

Trademark and Sources Referenced Disclaimer: All trademarks and trade names used or mentioned are the property of their respective owners and are used only to describe and provide specific examples. Every effort has been made to properly capitalize, punctuate, and attribute trademarks and trade names to their respective owners. Further, every effort has been made to cite all sources used in the compilation of this book.

First Edition

Website: **www.askmesmarter.com**

CONTENTS

Why AMS! - Language Arts, Social Studies, Science, and Math?

- Because it is a parent friendly, kid-engaging resource that reinforces what elementary-aged children are learning in school! It is presented as, *"just the facts, never mind the bells and whistles!"*

- Because the BRAIN cannot resist a question! *What color are your eyes?*

- Because learning is optimized through progressive questioning and spaced retention!

- Because it provides parents and teachers with a simplified and stream-lined format in interpreting an elementary school curriculum and prescribed learning targets! Most questions can be interpreted as *"I CAN"* statements per subject and grade level.

- Because it is a go-to supplemental resource for **HOME SCHOOLING** families!

- Because it serves as a comprehensive summer "**Bridge**" tool or "**road trip**" companion for reinforcing learned concepts, for preparing students for the next grade level, and for preventing the proverbial "SUMMER SLIDE!"

- Because it *aligns with state content standards and learning targets per subject and grade level* encompassing progressive CORE area questions and answers!

A Note to Parents

This comprehensive and progressive question and answer book is based on the premise that parents are their children's greatest and most influential educators!

It is designed as an **additional** tool to help parents and homeschool families empower their children with a solid knowledge foundation, *based on traditional state content standards* per grade level, as they progress through their elementary school years. It is intended to enhance and reinforce the facts, ideas, and concepts that children are already learning in school.

It serves to provide concrete questions that relate to the listed content standards per subject and per grade level. Many questions represent **"I CAN"** statements.

Knowledge gained by answering content questions is a sound learning strategy in that it is:

Specific
Measurable
Aligned to elementary state standards
Results-oriented
Time framed by grade level
Empowering
Reinforcing

Preface

This resource provides a **one-source** guide for parents to help their children reinforce important facts and concepts prescribed in an elementary curriculum in the four core areas. It further allows for review and reinforcement based on child-readiness and retention capacity.

Children have different learning rates and different learning styles. *The interrogation format is engaging for the young learner in that **the brain cannot resist a question!*** Further, the key to long-term retention is sustained practice over time.

This book also serves as a comprehensive resource for **home-schooling** families, a vacation or summer **"bridge"** tool for young learners when school is not in session, or a good companion during a long road trip!

Inherent in this simple question format is building a child's self-esteem with a *low-anxiety* verbal approach, empowering him or her with essential knowledge, facts, and insights.

What follows here in this book is a compilation of progressive questions aligned to curriculum standards in **LANGUAGE ARTS, SOCIAL STUDIES, SCIENCE, and MATH for 4th Grade.**

CORE Questions: It is given that many questions in this book could represent a full week lesson, many worksheets, practice, application, and analysis. In many cases, a choice is offered after a question, but this choice could easily be eliminated if need be, or if the question is asked for the second or third time.

LANGUAGE ARTS: Many of these questions encompass SIGHT words, spelling, phonics, readings, songs, rhymes, opposites, and essential grammar facts. **Specific 4th questions** include (**but not limited to**): reading and writing; parts of a story; paragraph and report writing; legends and myths; poetry; foreshowing; allegory; hyperbole; similes and metaphors; alliteration; onomatopoeia; abbreviations; research resources; colons; apostrophes; contractions; word stems; prefixes and suffixes; synonyms and antonyms; parts of speech;

contractions; idioms; declaratives, comparatives and superlatives; interrogatives; abbreviations; types of text; and **SIGHT** words.

SOCIAL STUDIES: Many of the social studies questions encompass geography, history, peoples, regions, and cultures. While many elementary schools may focus on different early civilizations, most do cover units relating to early American heritage and history. **Specific 4th questions** include (**but not limited to**): Earth; countries and continents; hemispheres; geographic regions; parallels and meridians; latitude and longitude; coordinates; mountain ranges; rivers, lakes, and oceans; deltas, straits, tributaries, peninsulas, and channels; grasslands and tablelands; canyons and basins; bays and gulfs; ancient civilizations; wonders of the world; U.S state facts and state nicknames; American symbols and documents; monuments and landmarks; Roman and Greek empires; Chinese dynasties; Medieval times; Egypt and Africa; world leaders; world religions; colonial America; the age of exploration; and U.S. government.

CIVICS: The focus of this chapter is to prompt children to think about all levels of government, the role of the citizen, and the importance of becoming contributing members of the community, the state, and the nation.

SCIENCE: The science questions encompass a wide array of scientific topics including astronomy, biology, chemistry, Earth science, ecology, geology, physics, weather/climate, and zoology. **Specific 4th questions** include (**but not limited to**): matter; atoms and molecules; elements; chemical and physical properties; basic substances; energy, motion, gravity, and force; simple machines; light; sound; cells; plant and animal kingdoms and classifications; organisms; Earth layers; waves; volcanos; rocks and minerals; weather, climate, and atmosphere; human body; and health. These learning standards can easily be applied to the outside world. Exploration and experimentation are highly encouraged!

MATH: The math questions encompass math skills, arithmetic, algebra, and geometry. **Specific 4th questions** include (**but not limited to**): place value; decimals; integers; Arabic and Roman numerals; rounding; prime and composite numbers; math properties; squares and square roots; inverse operations; order of operations; products and quotients; divisors and dividends; factorization; currency computation; time; measurement; Metric and U.S. Customary Units; fractions; line segments; shapes; polygons; angles; and mean, median, and mode. Allowing for paper and pencil computation, and actually *looking* at the math questions is encouraged if need be!

Questions are somewhat **sequential** and are inherently progressive as students gain knowledge. The questions are aimed to serve as a *representation* of what is listed as the prescribed "standards" or learning outcomes for the elementary grade levels in most states.

Many questions may be posed as **yes** and **no** or true and false questions, simply to suggest a specific learning objective. For many of the questions it is suggested that *similar* types of questions be asked to promote further competence and awareness. For example, a child may be asked to name something blue in his or her bedroom. You can follow up with, "What is found in nature that is blue?" A more advanced level question may ask the learner to name all the colors in the rainbow. (ROY G BIV)

In assessing correctness, the answers are located at the end of the book in **numerical order.**

Research shows that children learn in different ways and at different rates. This resource is formatted to compliment the brain networks that play a key role in learning. The "**Spacing Effect**" is a sound strategy in that facts are learned best when they are studied at frequent intervals over time.

As you use this question and answer book as a supplemental learning tool, it is important to keep in mind:

1) Many of the questions have a **choice** of answers after the colon. The degree of difficulty is inherent in these questions in that the choice can be read or not, at the discretion of the person asking the questions, and the readiness of the learner.

2) Many questions are **yes** or **no** questions that reflect a specific learning standard per grade level. These questions are given the answer "Yes" if only to suggest the learning goal.

3) Many of the questions asked in the higher grades are admittedly a *"stretch,"* but they are purposely included to challenge and engage the young learner.

4) **SUGGESTION:** SCAN the *answer list* if you need to target specific topics based on your scope, sequence, and your current theme. Also, you may want to **"bookmark"** the answer section that corresponds with the questions you are asking.

5) Feel free to use *your* unique creativity to *fancy up* and integrate these questions in a *child-engaging* format for your young learners!

AMS! - Making Knowledge **FUN** - da - men - tal!

"Knowledge is potential power!"

Now go ahead, ask them smarter!

CHAPTER 1

Language Arts – 4th Grade

1. What is the name of the general area that includes reading, writing, spelling, and composition: English or language arts?

2. Can you read silently?

3. Can you read aloud?

4. Can you summarize out loud something that you have read?

5. What is a short story that you have read?

6. What is a chapter book that you have read?

7. What is the name of a poem you have read?

8. Do all poems have rhyme?

9. What is the term for the division of lines in poetry: a stanza or a refrain?

10. What is the name of the verse or phrase that is repeated often in a poem or a song: a refrain or a chorus?

11. What is the term for the ordinary language that people use in speaking or writing that does not have the repeating rhythm that is used in verse: drama or prose?

12. What is the name of the short, lyric poem that originated in Italy: sonnet or prose?

13. How many lines does a **sonnet** have: twelve or fourteen?

14. What famous English writer wrote many sonnets: William Shakespeare or Edgar Allan Poe?

15. What is the name of a **play** that you have read?

16. Can you identify the title and the author of a book?

17. Where is the **Table of Contents** located in a book?

18. Where is the **index** located in a book?

19. What do you use an index for: to look up the meaning of a word, or to find the page number that the topic is on?

20. What is the name of the **dictionary** section of a textbook: an index or a glossary?

21. What is the name of the beginning part that is written by the *author* to introduce the book: the foreword or the preface?

22. What is the name given for the written addition at the end of the book: the preface or the appendix?

23. Can you use a print or online dictionary to look up the meaning of a word?

24. What is another purpose for using a dictionary besides looking up the meaning of a word?

25. What do you say when you answer the telephone?

26. Can you make a prediction about what a story is about before reading it?

27. Can you put all the events of a story in the proper sequence?

28. Can you identify the main idea in a narrative text?

29. Can you state the author's purpose when reading text?

30. Can you state the supporting details when reading text?

31. Can you compare two stories and say how they are similar?

32. How do "Cinderella" and "Sleeping Beauty" compare?

33. Can you contrast two stories and say how they are different?

34. How do "Cinderella" and "Sleeping Beauty" contrast?

35. What is the name for the action that occurs in a story that makes something else happen: compare and contrast or cause and effect?

36. Which sentence is the cause and which sentence is the effect: "Pluto is one of the coldest planets." and, "Pluto is the farthest planet from the sun?"

37. What is the name of the reading genre that uses characters, plots, and settings to convey events that are **not** true?

38. What is the name of the reading genre that uses real people, plots, and settings to convey actual events that **are** true?

39. What is the name of the reading genre that uses **animals** who act and speak like people and that teaches a moral lesson: a fable or a folktale?

40. Which author is famous for writing the fables: *"The Tortoise and the Hare"* and *"The Boy Who Cried Wolf:"* Aesop or Shakespeare?

41. What is the name of the reading genre that is a made-up story with folk heroes like "Paul Bunyan," and "Pecos Bill," and is passed down from one generation to the next: a tall tale or a myth?

42. What is the name for the story that is presented with dialogue and action: drama or prose?

43. What is the name of an account of someone's life that is written by another person: a biography or a bibliography?

44. What is the name of a traditional story that has been passed down from person to person like *"Robin Hood,"* and has important meaning: a legend or a fairy tale?

45. Is *"Sleepy Hollow"* by Washington Irving an example of a legend?

46. Is *"King Arthur and the Knights of the Round Table"* an English legend or an Irish legend?

47. Is *"Robin Hood"* an English legend or an Irish legend?

48. What is the name of a story that often includes gods and heroes as in *"Zeus"* and *"Pandora's Box:"* a myth or a legend?

49. Is *"Hercules"* an example of a Greek myth or a Roman myth?

50. What is the name of a narrative poem that has a refrain, tells a story, and is often sung: a ballad or a limerick?

51. What is the name of a five-line humorous poem originating from Ireland whereby lines 1, 2, and 5 rhyme as in *"There Once Was a Man from Nantucket*:" a limerick or a sonnet?

52. What is the name for the literary device found in many works of literature that uses ridicule or sarcasm aimed at someone or something, and is evident in many political cartoons: satire or epic?

53. What is the name for the story in which the events and characters are symbols that stand for truths about something in life and teach a lesson as in *"Moby Dick*:" an allegory or a limerick?

54. What is the name for an extended literary poem that has been passed down from ancient civilizations that celebrates the feats of a legendary hero as in, *"The Iliad," "The Odyssey," "Beowulf,"* and Dante's *"The Divine Comedy:"* lyrical poem or epic poem?

55. What is the term that includes plot, theme, characters, and setting: literary elements or story line?

56. What is the literary term called when you use the clues in the text to get a sense of what will happen next: foreshadowing or predicting?

57. What is the name of the literary term that is an extreme exaggeration of what something really is: allegory or hyperbole?

58. What is the term for the figure of speech that compares two unlike things as in *"cheeks like roses:"* a simile or a metaphor?

59. What is the term for the figure of speech that compares two unlike things *without* using the words like or as: a simile or a metaphor?

60. Is the phrase, **"their cheeks were roses"** a simile or a metaphor?

61. What is the literary term for a sentence in poetry where several of the words start with the same consonant as in Peter Piper Picked a Peck of Pickled Peppers: alliteration or onomatopoeia?

62. What is the literary term given for the sound we say something makes as in *"The snake hissed," "The bee buzzed,"* or, *"The wolf howled at the moon:"* onomatopoeia or alliteration?

63. What is the literary term when human qualities are given to objects or animals as in, *"this city never sleeps," "the stars winked at me,"* and *"lightning danced across the sky:"* alliteration or personification?

64. How do you finish the saying: **"Beauty is only skin_?"**

65. How do you finish the saying: "The bigger they are, the harder they_?"

66. How do you finish the saying: **"Bull in a china _?"**

67. How do you finish the saying: *"Bury the _?"*

68. How do you finish the saying: *"Make ends _?"*

69. How do you finish the saying: *"Don't put all your eggs in one _?"*

70. How do you finish the saying: *"Don't count your chickens before they_?"*

71. How do you finish the saying: *"One picture is worth a thousand _?"*

72. How do you finish the saying: *"Two wrongs don't make a _?"*

73. How do you finish the saying: *"Can't hold a candle _?"*

74. How do you finish the saying: *"Seeing is _?"*

75. How do you finish the saying: *"Half a loaf is better than _?"*

76. How do you finish the saying: *"Haste makes _?"*

77. How do you finish the saying: "Lightning never strikes twice in the same _?"

78. How do you finish the saying: *"Once in a blue _?"*

79. How do you finish the saying: *"An ounce of prevention is worth a pound of _?"*

80. How do you finish the saying: *"When it rains it _?"*

81. How do you finish the saying: *"Live and let_?"*

82. How do you finish the saying: *"Through thick and_?"*

83. How do you finish the saying: *"You can lead a horse to water, but you can't make it __?"*

84. What is **etc.** an abbreviation for that means "and so on?"

85. What is the French abbreviation that is often included on a written invitation when the person writing the invitation wishes for a response, and is short for, *Répondez S'il Vous Plaît*?

86. Can you print using both upper case and lowercase letters?

87. Are you developing your skill in writing in cursive?

88. Can you write a letter to a friend or to a family member?

89. Can you write an email?

90. Can you write a poem?

91. Can you write a report about a topic that interests you?

92. If you use written ideas from a source, what do you need to include in your report that gives credit to the author of that source: a biography or a bibliography?

93. What information would be included in a bibliography?

94. What is the alphabetical order of the bibliography: author's first name or author's last name?

95. Can you write a book report?

96. Can you write a description of a holiday, an object, or a person?

97. Can you write a thank you note?

98. Can you outline the main points from something that you have read?

99. Can you write a written summary of something that you have read?

100. Can you write a summary of what you did today?

101. What is the name of the process that includes pre-writing, drafting, revising, editing, and publishing: writing or proofreading?

102. What is the name of your first attempt to write down all of your ideas in an essay format, after you have at put together all of your thoughts: rough draft or outline?

103. What is the first sentence of a paragraph called that tells us what the main idea of the paragraph is: a thesis statement or a topic sentence?

104. What is the sentence called at the end of a paragraph: a topic sentence or a concluding sentence?

105. Can you write a concluding paragraph at the end of a report?

106. What is the name of a story that you write that includes a plot, setting, point of view, conflict, and has a closing paragraph at the end: prose or drama?

107. Do you use transitional words in your writing like next, finally, and in conclusion?

108. Do you include several descriptive adjectives and verbs in your writing?

109. Can you write something to persuade, inform, and entertain?

110. What could you write about to persuade someone to do something?

111. What could you write about to inform someone about something?

112. What could you write about to entertain someone?

113. Can you write a reflective *response* to literature, making a judgment about what you read?

114. What resources could you use if you were writing a *research paper*?

115. What resource would you look in to find basic information about frogs: an almanac, a thesaurus, or an encyclopedia?

116. What resource would you look in to find a synonym for *delicious*: a dictionary or a thesaurus?

117. What resource would you look at to find the meaning of *concave*: a dictionary or a thesaurus?

118. What resource would you look at to find the longitude of *Sweden*: an atlas or an almanac?

119. What resource would you look at to find information about the *Aztec* culture: an almanac or an online encyclopedia?

120. Do you have basic computer keyboard skills for typing a paper or a report?

121. Does learning grammar include being familiar with the parts of speech? *(Noun, verb, etc.)*

122. What is the name of the grammatical construction in which a noun is followed by another noun, e.g., **"My uncle, the doctor…"** that helps to explain it: apposition or alliteration?

123. How many parts of speech are there in the English language: eight or twelve?

124. What *major* part of speech is missing in the following list: Noun, adjective, pronoun, adverb, preposition, conjunction, and interjection?

125. What part of speech refers to a person, animal, place, thing, or idea?

126. What is the **noun** in the sentence: "The cheetah ran swiftly?"

127. What part of speech describes or *modifies* a noun: a pronoun or an adjective?

128. What is the **adjective** in the sentence: "Rusty is a smart dog?"

129. What part of speech takes the place of a noun: a pronoun or an adjective?

130. What is the **pronoun** is the sentence: "He is a smart dog?"

131. What pronoun would take the place of *Alex*?

132. What pronoun would take the place of *Rebecca*?

133. What pronoun would replace *the car*?

134. What pronoun would replace *Andrew and Zachary*?

135. Are the words I, she, he, and it considered *personal* pronouns or *possessive* pronouns?

136. Are the words mine, yours, his, hers, ours considered *personal* pronouns or *possessive* pronouns?

137. What part of speech describes the **main** action in a sentence?

138. What is the **verb** in the sentence, "I jumped over the rock?"

139. Do all sentences have a subject and a verb?

140. What part of speech tells *how* an action occurred: an adjective or an adverb?

141. What is the **adverb** in the sentence: "He ran quickly to the park?"

142. What is the **adverb** in the sentence: "Emily plays the piano well?"

143. What is the name for the part of speech that shows location and **links** nouns, pronouns, and phrases to the other parts of a sentence: conjunction or preposition?

144. Are the words *in, at, around, to, through, toward,* and *above* considered conjunctions or prepositions?

145. What is the **preposition** in the sentence: "The alarm clock is beside the bed?"

146. What is the **preposition** in the sentence: "My jacket is on the chair?"

147. Are the phrases, *over the hill, behind the door,* and *outside the house* prepositional phrases or adverbial phrases?

148. What part of speech *joins* words or phrases in a sentence: an interjection or a conjunction?

149. What is the **conjunction** in the sentence: "I sold cakes and cookies?"

150. What is the **conjunction** in the sentence: "I wanted to go but I had to study?"

151. What part of speech is included in a sentence for effect and emphasis: an interjection or a conjunction?

152. What is the **interjection** in this sentence: "Wow! That was a great show?"

153. Does a *complete* sentence include a subject and a predicate?

154. Does a *clause* contain both a subject and a verb?

155. What is the subject in the sentence: "Jack loves ice cream?"

156. What is the predicate in the sentence: "Jack loves ice cream?"

157. What kind of sentence would you have if you left out a predicate or a subject: a run-on or a fragment?

158. Is the sentence, "Visited Disneyworld last year" a fragment or a run-on?

159. What word could you add to the beginning of "Visited Disneyworld" to make it a complete sentence?

160. Is the sentence, *"I went to Chicago it is a big city"* a fragment or a run-on sentence?

161. How can we divide the sentence, *"I went to Chicago it is a big city"* into two separate sentences?

162. How would you combine the following run-on sentence to make one sentence? *Lisa made cookies. Michael made cookies.*

163. What is the correct **verb form** in the sentence: "I am /are tall?"

164. What is the correct **verb form** in the sentence: "He is /are funny?

165. What is the correct **verb form** in the sentence: "They is /are outside?"

166. What is the correct **verb form** in the sentence: "My friend Nathan live /lives in Ohio?"

167. What is the correct **verb form** in the sentence: "A pack of wolves was /were running through the woods?"

168. What kind of sentence is in the form of a **statement:** a declarative or an imperative?

169. What kind of sentence is in the form of a **question**: an interrogative or a declarative?

170. What kind of sentence expresses strong **feelings**: a declarative or an exclamatory?

171. What kind of sentence gives instructions or expresses a **command:** declarative or imperative?

172. What kind of sentence is, *"It is windy today:"* a declarative, an imperative, an interrogative, or an exclamatory sentence?

173. What punctuation mark does a declarative sentence end with?

174. What kind of sentence is, *"Are you going to the party:"* a declarative, an imperative, an interrogative, or an exclamatory sentence?

175. What punctuation mark does an interrogative sentence end with?

176. How do you say the sentence, *"The game is over."* with an interrogative voice?

177. How do you say the sentence, *"The game is over."* with a declarative voice?

178. What kind of sentence is, **"We won the championship:"** a declarative, an imperative, an interrogative, or an exclamatory sentence?

179. What punctuation mark does an imperative sentence often end with?

180. What kind of sentence is similar to a command or an order: declarative or imperative?

181. What kind of sentence is, *"Go walk the dog:"* a declarative, an imperative, an interrogative, or an exclamatory?

182. What punctuation mark tells a reader when to pause in a sentence?

183. Where is the **comma** placed in the date *December 7 1949*?

184. Where is the **comma** placed in the sentence, *"Yes you may go the park?"*

185. Where is the **comma** placed when you address an envelope to *Orlando FL?*

186. Is a comma place before or after the quotation marks in the dialog phrase, "*I have a surprise for you,*" said Brian?

187. Is a comma place before or after the conjunctions "and" or "but," when connecting two independent clauses?

188. Where is the **comma** placed in the sentence, "Sticks and stones may break my bones but words can never hurt me?"

189. What separates items that are listed in a series of two or more: periods or commas?

190. Where are the commas placed in the sentence, "Samantha brought cookies brownies and cupcakes to sell at the bake sale?"

191. What is the correct punctuation mark when introducing a list of ideas, or setting off a quotation: a comma or a colon?

192. What is the punctuation mark that looks like a dot with a comma underneath it that is used to separate parts of a sentence, or to separate main clauses: a colon or a semi-colon?

193. What is the punctuation mark that looks like two dots that is used to call attention to what follows such as a list or an explanation: a colon or a semi-colon?

194. What punctuation mark do you use after the greeting *Dear Sirs* in a business letter: a semi-colon or a colon?

195. What punctuation mark do you use after *Dear Krista* in a personal letter: a colon or a comma?

196. What punctuation mark do you use between the hours and the minutes when writing the time *six fifteen*: a comma or a colon?

197. What punctuation mark do you use between a title and a sub-title: a colon or a semi-colon?

198. What is the name of the punctuation mark that is used to show possession: an apostrophe or a comma?

199. Where is the **apostrophe** placed in the phrase, **My friends house**: before or after the s? *(sing.)*

200. Is the apostrophe placed before or after the **"s"** if the noun is already plural and ends in the letter "s?"

201. Where is the apostrophe placed in the sentence: **"The girls** *(plural)* **room was a mess?"**

202. Where is the apostrophe placed in the phrase: **"The dogs** *(singular)* **house?"**

203. What is the name of the punctuation mark used in a contraction: a comma or an apostrophe?

204. What can an apostrophe take the place of in a contraction: letters or words?

205. Where is the apostrophe placed to make the contraction meaning **we are** from *w-e-r-e*?

206. What letter is the apostrophe replacing in the contraction *we're*?

207. What letter is the apostrophe replacing in the contraction *isn't*?

208. What is the contraction for the words *do not*?

209. What is the contraction for the words *I would*?

210. What is the contraction for the words *they are*?

211. What two words make up the contraction *she's*?

212. What two words make up the contraction *I'll*?

213. What two words make up the contraction *you're*?

214. What two words make up the contraction *didn't*?

215. What two words make up the contraction *won't*?

216. What do you call the punctuation marks that are used in text to indicate the *exact* words of the speaker?

217. Are the titles of poems, articles, and short stories set off in quotation marks?

218. Where would the quotation marks be placed in the following sentence: *I have a game tonight, said Jordan?*

219. What is a word called that means the **same** thing as another word: a synonym or an antonym?

220. What is a synonym of **spotless**?

221. What is a synonym of **buddy**?

222. What is a synonym of **attempt**?

223. What is a synonym of **lady**?

224. What is a synonym of **strange**?

225. What is a synonym of **happy**?

226. What is a word called that means the *opposite* of another word: a synonym or an antonym?

227. What is an antonym of **fail**?

228. What is an antonym of **true**?

229. What is an antonym of **cheap**?

230. What is an antonym of **sunny**?

231. What is an antonym of **liquid**?

232. What is an antonym of **out-going**?

233. What is an antonym of **wet**?

234. What is an antonym of **near**?

235. What is an antonym of **over**?

236. What is an antonym of **soft**?

237. What is an antonym of **rough**?

238. What are groups of letters called that are added to the *beginning* of a word to form a new word that has a different meaning: a suffix or a prefix?

239. What is the meaning of the prefixes **non-, im-,** and **in-**: not or wrong?

240. What is the prefix of the word *impossible*?

241. What is the meaning of the word *impossible*?

242. What is the prefix of the word *invisible*?

243. What is the meaning of the word *invisible*?

244. What is the prefix of the word *nonfiction*?

245. What is the meaning of the word *nonfiction*?

246. What is the meaning of the prefix <u>mis</u>-: not or wrong?

247. What is the prefix of the word *misbehave*?

248. What is the meaning of the word *misbehave*?

249. What is the meaning of the prefix <u>pre</u>-: before or after?

250. What is the prefix of the word *pregame*?

251. What is the meaning of the word *pregame*?

252. What is the meaning of the prefix <u>en</u>-: out or in?

253. What is the prefix in the word *endanger*?

254. What is the meaning of the word *endanger*?

255. Are suffixes added to the beginning or to the end of a word?

256. What **suffix** is often used to form an adverb: -ly or -ful?

257. What is the suffix in the adverb *swiftly*?

258. What suffix can you add to the adjective *easy* to make it an adverb: -ly or -ily?

259. What suffix can you add to the word *sleep* to make it an adjective: -ly or-y?

260. What is the meaning of the suffix -**ful**: capable of or full of?

261. What is the suffix in the word *playful*?

262. What is the meaning of the suffix -**able** or -**ible:** capable of or full of?

263. What is the suffix of the word *washable*?

264. What is the suffix of the word *flexible*?

265. Is the suffix *–ment* used to turn a verb into a noun or a noun into a verb?

266. What suffix is added to the verb *agree* to make it a noun?

267. By removing the suffix, how would you change the word *achievement* from a noun to a verb?

268. What is the name of the word that does *not* have a prefix or suffix: a stem word or a Latin word?

269. What is the stem of the word *undeniable*?

270. What is the term given to a word that is spelled the same in both directions, e.g. eye, pop, kayak, madam, deed, level, radar, and racecar: a palindrome or a homophone?

271. What is the term for a phrase whose meaning cannot be directly understood from the meaning of the words contained in it as in, *"You are pulling my leg:"* a homophone or an idiom?

272. Would a person who does not speak fluent English have an easy or hard time understanding idioms?

273. Can you recognize and pronounce the common sight word "**action**?" (Show word)

274. Can you recognize and pronounce the common sight word "**actually**?" (Show word)

275. Can you recognize and pronounce the common sight word "**alive**?" (Show word)

276. Can you recognize and pronounce the common sight word "**although**?" (Show word)

277. Can you recognize and pronounce the common sight word "**amount**?" (Show word)

278. Can you recognize and pronounce the common sight word "**area**?" (Show word)

279. Can you recognize and pronounce the common sight word "**blood**?" (Show word)

280. Can you recognize and pronounce the common sight word "**cause**?" (Show word)

281. Can you recognize and pronounce the common sight word "**central**?" (Show word)

282. Can you recognize and pronounce the common sight word "**century**?" (Show word)

283. Can you recognize and pronounce the common sight word "**charcoal**?" (Show word)

284. Can you recognize and pronounce the common sight word "**chart**?" (Show word)

285. Can you recognize and pronounce the common sight word "**check**?" (Show word)

286. Can you recognize and pronounce the common sight word "**club**?" (Show word)

287. Can you recognize and pronounce the common sight word "**colony**?" (Show word)

288. Can you recognize and pronounce the common sight word "**company**?" (Show word)

289. Can you recognize and pronounce the common sight word "**condition**?" (Show word)

290. Can you recognize and pronounce the common sight word "**court**?" (Show word)

291. Can you recognize and pronounce the common sight word "**deal**?" (Show word)

292. Can you recognize and pronounce the common sight word "**death**?" (Show word)

293. Can you recognize and pronounce the common sight word "**describe**?" (Show word)

294. Can you recognize and pronounce the common sight word "**design**?" (Show word)

295. Can you recognize and pronounce the common sight word "**disease**?" (Show word)

296. Can you recognize and pronounce the common sight word "**eleven**?" (Show word)

297. Can you recognize and pronounce the common sight word "**equal**?" (Show word)

298. Can you recognize and pronounce the common sight word "**experience**?" (Show word)

299. Can you recognize and pronounce the common sight word "**factor**?" (Show word)

300. Can you recognize and pronounce the common sight word "**favorite**?" (Show word)

301. Can you recognize and pronounce the common sight word "**figure**?" (Show word)

302. Can you recognize and pronounce the common sight word "**hospital**?" (Show word)

303. Can you recognize and pronounce the common sight word "**include**?" (Show word)

304. Can you recognize and pronounce the common sight word "**increase**?" (Show word)

305. Can you recognize and pronounce the common sight word "**known**?" (Show word)

306. Can you recognize and pronounce the common sight word "**least**?" (Show word)

307. Can you recognize and pronounce the common sight word "**length**?" (Show word)

308. Can you recognize and pronounce the common sight word "**loud**?" (Show word)

309. Can you recognize and pronounce the common sight word "**measure**?" (Show word)

310. Can you recognize and pronounce the common sight word "**molecule**?" (Show word)

311. Can you recognize and pronounce the common sight word "**national**?" (Show word)

312. Can you recognize and pronounce the common sight word "**necessary**?" (Show word)

313. Can you recognize and pronounce the common sight word "**noun**?" (Show word)

314. Can you recognize and pronounce the common sight word "**oxygen**?" (Show word)

315. Can you recognize and pronounce the common sight word "**phrase**?" (Show word)

316. Can you recognize and pronounce the common sight word "**property**?" (Show word)

317. Can you recognize and pronounce the common sight word "**radio**?" (Show word)

318. Can you recognize and pronounce the common sight word "**receive**?" (Show word)

319. Can you recognize and pronounce the common sight word "**replace**?" (Show word)

320. Can you recognize and pronounce the common sight word "**rhythm**?" (Show word)

321. Can you recognize and pronounce the common sight word "**serve**?" (Show word)

322. Can you recognize and pronounce the common sight word "**similar**?" (Show word)

323. Can you recognize and pronounce the common sight word "**southern**?" (Show word)

324. Can you recognize and pronounce the common sight word "**squirrel**?" (Show word)

325. Can you recognize and pronounce the common sight word "**straight**?" (Show word)

326. Can you recognize and pronounce the common sight word "**subtle**?" (Show word)

327. Can you recognize and pronounce the common sight word "**suffix**?" (Show word)

328. Can you recognize and pronounce the common sight word "**surely**?" (Show word)

329. Can you recognize and pronounce the common sight word "**though**?" (Show word)

330. Can you recognize and pronounce the common sight word "**thought**?" (Show word)

331. Can you recognize and pronounce the common sight word "**touch**?" (Show word)

332. Can you recognize and pronounce the common sight word "**twice**?" (Show word)

333. Can you recognize and pronounce the common sight word "**used**?" (Show word)

334. Can you recognize and pronounce the common sight word "**usually**?" (Show word)

335. Can you recognize and pronounce the common sight word "**view**?" (Show word)

336. Can you recognize and pronounce the common sight word "**weight**?" (Show word)

337. Can you recognize and pronounce the common sight word "**wheat**?" (Show word)

338. Can you recognize and pronounce the common sight word "**whom**?" (Show word)

339. Can you recognize and pronounce the common sight word "**young**?" (Show word)

CHAPTER 2

Social Studies – 4th Grade

1. What is the name of the planet we live on?

2. What is the name for the *spherical* representation of the Earth?

3. How many continents are on planet Earth?

4. What are the two main oceans on planet Earth?

5. Which of the seven continents can you name?

6. Can you read a map?

7. What are *climate, economic, physical, road, political,* and *topographic* all considered?

8. What is the name of the *imaginary line* that divides the globe in half and runs east to west?

9. What is the name of the *imaginary line* that divides the globe in half and runs north to south: the equator or the prime meridian?

10. What is the name for the top sphere and the bottom sphere of the Earth: globe or hemisphere?

11. How many hemispheres is the Earth divided into?

12. What is the geographical term given for everything *above* the equator: Northern Hemisphere or Southern Hemisphere?

13. What is the geographical term given for everything *below* the equator: Northern Hemisphere or Southern Hemisphere?

14. What is the geographical term given for everything to the *right* of the Prime Meridian: Eastern Hemisphere or Western Hemisphere?

15. What is the geographical term given for everything to the *left* of the Prime Meridian: Eastern Hemisphere or Western Hemisphere?

16. What is the name of the imaginary line that divides the globe down the middle at the poles: the equator or the prime meridian?

17. What two hemispheres does the **prime meridian** divide: Northern and Southern, or Eastern and Western?

18. What is the name for the lines that run **parallel** to the equator: parallels or meridians?

19. What is the name for the lines that run from pole to pole: parallels or meridians?

20. What is the name of the geographic coordinate that runs north to south: latitude or longitude?

21. What is the name of the geographic coordinate that runs east to west: latitude or longitude?

22. Do lines of latitude run north or south or east to west?

23. Do lines of longitude run north to south or east to west?

24. What is the name for the point where lines of longitude are measured from: the prime meridian or the equator?

25. What is the name of the place in *England* that measures zero degrees longitude: London or Greenwich?

26. Do all parallels and meridians have a number?

27. What is the name of the unit of measurement for longitude and latitude: coordinate or degree?

28. What is the *degree* number of the equator at the eastern most point and the western most point, and at the intersection with the Prime Meridian: 0 or 90?

29. What is the degree number of the Prime Meridian from North Pole to South Pole: 90 or 180?

30. What is another name for the 180th meridian, halfway around the globe: the Prime Meridian or the International Dateline?

31. What is the name for where meridians and parallels intersect: an axis or a coordinate?

32. How would you read the coordinates 30 degrees North 20 degrees east: 30 degrees north of the equator and 20 degrees east of the prime meridian, or 30 degrees north of the prime meridian and 20 degrees east of the equator?

33. When given the exact coordinates of a place, can you find the location of that place on a map?

34. Can you identify several states while looking at a map of the United States?

35. Can you identify *your* city and several others on a state map?

36. Can you follow a map inside a building?

37. What is the term for the *proportion* between the distance on a map and the real distance on the Earth's surface: scope or scale?

38. Do most maps include *scales* on the bottom or in the corner?

39. What kind of map might you be looking at if the scale reads one inch equal one hundred miles: a city map or a state map?

40. What kind of map might you be looking at if the scale reads one inch is equal to one mile: a state map or a city map?

41. What kind of map might you be looking at if the scale reads one inch is equal to 1,000 miles: a state map or a country map?

42.   What is the name for the type of map that shows the outlines of the 48 states with their capitals in the continental United States: a political map or a relief map?

43.   What is the name for the type of map that shows the landscape like hills, mountains, and rivers: a political map or a relief map?

44.   What is the name for the type of map that shows the original 13 colonies or battles of the Civil War: a political map or a historical map?

45.   What is the name for the type of map that shows hills and valleys with contour lines, and is often three-dimensional: a relief map or a physical map?

46.   What is the name for the type of map that shows the distribution of natural resources: a physical map or a resource map?

47.   What is the name for the type of map that shows pictures of cheese in the state of Wisconsin and pictures of oranges in the state of Florida: a relief map or a product map?

48.   What is the name for the type of map that shows highways, airports, railroad tracks, cities, and points of interest: a guide map or a road map?

49.   What is the name for the type of map that shows information about the temperatures and precipitation of a region: a climate map or a topographic map?

50.   What is the name for the type of map that shows the elevations of different areas by using lines drawn close together to indicate steep terrain, and lines drawn far apart to indicate flat terrain, a political map or a topographic map?

51. What is the name for the type of map that indicates the locations of the major mountain ranges: a relief map or a topographic map?

52. What is the name of the mountain range in North America stretching 3,000 miles from New Mexico through Colorado and Canada, and north to Alaska: the Rockies or the Appalachians?

53. What is the name of the **tallest** mountain peak in Alaska: Mount Everest or Mount McKinley?

54. What is the name of the mountain range in North America stretching 1,800 miles from Alabama to the Gulf of Saint Lawrence that include the White Mountains, the Allegheny Mountains, the Blue Ridge Mountains, and the Great Smoky Mountains: the Rocky Mountains or the Appalachian Mountains?

55. Which mountain range has taller peaks: the Appalachians or the Rockies?

56. Which mountain range is **older**: the Appalachians or the Rockies?

57. What natural things occurred that explains why the Appalachians, over 280 million years old, are shorter and have less jagged peaks than the Rockies, over 130 million years old?

58. What does the state of **Montana** translate to from Spanish to English?

59. What is the name of the mountain range in South America, the **longest** mountain range in the world, stretching 4,500 miles from the Caribbean coast to the southern tip of the continent: the Andes Mountains or the Ural Mountains?

60. What is the name of the *highest* mountain in the **Andes** that measures over 22,000 feet above sea level: Mount Everest or Mount Aconcagua?

61. What ancient Indian civilization settled in the Andes of Peru with Cusco as their capital city: the Aztecs or the Incas?

62. What is the name of the city built by the Incas high in the Andes Mountains, 8,000 feet above sea level that was re-discovered by Hiram Bingham in 1911: Tenochtitlan or Machu Picchu?

63. What is the name of the mountain range located along the northwest coast of Africa stretching 1,500 miles: The Atlas Mountains or the Eastern Highlands?

64. What is the name of the mountain range located in Eastern Africa: The Atlas Mountains or the Eastern Highlands?

65. What is the name of the *tallest volcanic mountain* in Africa: Mount Kilimanjaro or Mount Kenya?

66. What is the name of the mountains that cover the European countries of Switzerland, Austria, France, and Italy: the Rockies or the Alps?

67. In which mountain range was a frozen human body, estimated to be 5,000 years old, discovered by hikers in 1991 and named "Otzi," the Ice Man: the Rockies or the Alps?

68. What is the name of the highest mountain in the French Alps in Europe meaning, *"White Mountain"* in English: Mont Blanc or Mont Fuji?

69. What is the name of the mountain range in **Russia** extending from the Arctic to the Caspian Sea: The Atlas Mountains or the Ural Mountains?

70. What is the name of the highest mountain in **Japan**: Mount Fuji or Mount Kilimanjaro?

71. What is the name of the tallest mountain range in the world: the Rockies or the Himalayas?

72. What is the name of the world's tallest mountain, measuring over 29,000 feet tall that is located between Nepal and Tibet in the Himalayas: Mount McKinley or Mount Everest?

73. What mountain peak was first conquered by Edmund Hillary and Tenzing Norgay in 1953: Mount McKinley or Mount Everest?

74. Is there more oxygen or less oxygen is you climb *higher* above sea level?

75. What are the **two** major mountain ranges in the continental United States?

76. Can the United States be divided into geographic regions?

77. What is the name of the **region** that refers to the states of Delaware, the District of Colombia, Maryland, New Jersey, New York, and Pennsylvania: Mid-Atlantic or Midwest?

78. What is the name of the **region** that refers to the states of Illinois, Iowa, Indiana, Kansas, Michigan, Minnesota, Missouri, Nebraska, North Dakota, Ohio, South Dakota, and Wisconsin: the Midwest or the Northwest?

79. What is the name of the **region** that refers to the states of Alaska, California, Hawaii, Oregon, and Washington: Northwestern States or the Pacific Northwest?

80. What is the name of the **region** that refers to the states of Arizona, Colorado, Idaho, Montana, Nevada, New Mexico, Utah, and Wyoming: Rocky Mountain or Pacific Northwest?

81.   What is the name of the **region** that refers to the states of Connecticut, Maine, Massachusetts, New Hampshire, Rhode Island, and Vermont: Atlantic States or New England?

82.   What is the name of the **region** that refers to the states of Florida, Georgia, North Carolina, South Carolina, and Virginia: South Atlantic States or Mid-Atlantic States?

83.   What is the name of the **region** that refers to the states of Arizona, California, Colorado, Nevada, New Mexico, and Utah: the Southwest or the Pacific Northwest?

84.   What is the name of the country *north* of the United States?

85.   What is the name of the country *south* of the United States?

86.   What are the two states that are located *outside* the continental United States?

87.   What type of map can you find landforms such as rivers, channels, deltas, and peninsulas: a political map or a relief map?

88.   What is the geographical term for a wide *waterway* between two landmasses like the one that is located at the Columbus River in Oregon: a strait or a channel?

89.   What is the geographical term for the navigable narrow waterway between two landmasses like the *Bering* located between Alaska and Siberia that connects the Pacific with the Arctic, or *Gibraltar* connecting the Atlantic with the Mediterranean: a delta or a strait?

90.   What is the geographical term for a landform that is formed at the *mouth* of a river from the deposition of sediment like the one in Northern Egypt where the Nile River spreads out and drains into the Mediterranean Sea: a channel or a delta?

91. What is the geographical term for a large expanse of grassland and flowers: a mesa or a prairie?

92. What is the geographical term for a tableland or high plain that is relatively level like those located in Tibet, Antarctic, and Colorado: a mesa or a plateau?

93. What is the geographical term for a hill with *steep* sides and a *flat* top like those found in Colorado and New Mexico: a mesa or a tableland?

94. What is the geographical term for a *steep* face of rock, ice, or Earth: a hill or a cliff?

95. What is the term for a *deep valley* with steep cliffs cut into the terrain by running water: a basin or a canyon?

96. What is the name of the famous **canyon**, considered by many to be one of the seven wonders of the natural world, located on the Colorado River in the state of Arizona?

97. What is the geographical term for a landform in the ocean or on land that is lower in the center than at the edges: a canyon or a basin?

98. What is the geographical term for a piece of land stretching out into water as a peninsula or a point: a cape or a gulf?

99. What is the name of the famous cape in the state of Massachusetts: Cape Cod or Boston Cape?

100. What is the geographical term for a large area of ocean that is *partially* enclosed by land: a gulf or a bay?

101. What is the name of the largest *gulf* in the world that is surrounded by Mexico, the United States, and Cuba?

102. What is the name of the **gulf** located between Saudi Arabia and Iran where petroleum is transferred on oil tankers: The Middle Eastern Gulf or the Persian Gulf?

103. What is the geographical term for a small body of water that is set off from a larger body of water where the land curves like San Francisco, Chesapeake, and Hudson: a bay or a gulf?

104. What is the geographical term for a dry, sandy area where cacti grow, tumbleweeds roll, and has very little rainfall?

105. What is the name of the biggest **desert** in the world that stretches across most of North Africa: the Sahara or Death Valley?

106. What is the name of the continent that is also considered a *polar* desert: Antarctica or Arctic?

107. What is the name of the desert that is named for a Native American tribe that stretches across California, Utah, Arizona, and Nevada and includes the area known as **"Death Valley:"** the Sonoran or the Mojave?

108. What is the name of the *driest* desert in the world that is located in Argentina and Chile in South America: the Atacama or the Arabian?

109. What is the name of the second largest desert in the world, located in Western Asia: the Arabian or the Atacama?

110. What is the geographical term for a part of land that extends into the water and is connected to the mainland by an isthmus, and include the Iberian, Yucatan, Italian, and the states of Florida and Alaska: a delta or a peninsula?

111. What is the geographical term for a *narrow* piece of land that connects two larger land masses like the bridge located in Panama that connects Central America with South America: a fjord or an isthmus?

112. What is the geographical term for an *inlet in the sea* between steep slopes carved out by a glacier, like those found in

Iceland, Norway, New Zealand, and the state of Alaska: an isthmus or a fjord?

113. What is the geographical term for a relatively **still** body of water that is surrounded by land: a river or a lake?

114. What is the geographical term for a *flowing* body of water that typically feeds into another body of water: a river or a lake?

115. What famous lakes can you name?

116. What are the names of the *five great lakes* in the United States whose initials spell out **H-O-M-E-S?**

117. What is the name of the shallow, salty lake in the state of Utah: Utah Lake or Great Salt Lake?

118. What famous rivers can you name in the world?

119. What famous rivers can you name in the United States?

120. What is the name of the 1,800 mile-long river that translate *"Big River"* in Spanish, and flows along the border between Texas and Mexico into the Gulf of Mexico?

121. What is the name of the second largest river in the world that is 4,000 miles long located in South America: the Nile or the Amazon?

122. What is the name of the **longest** river in the world that is 4,150 miles long, flowing northward through Eastern Africa into the Mediterranean: The Yellow or the Nile?

123. What is the name of the second longest river in that is 2,800 miles long located in **China**: the Ganges or the Yellow?

124. What is the name of the longest river in **Asia** that flows from Tibet into the East China Sea at Shanghai: the Ganges or the Yangtze?

125. What river located in Asia is 1,550 miles long, flows from the Himalayas into the Bay of Bengal, and is regarded as *sacred* by the Hindus: the Ganges or the Yangtze?

126. What is the name of the longest river in Europe and one of **Russia's** most important rivers: the Volga or the Yellow?

127. What is the second longest river in Europe that is 1,725 miles long, borders ten countries, and flows from Southeastern Germany into the Black Sea: The Yellow or the Danube?

128. What is the name of the major river in Germany besides the Danube: The Yellow or the Rhine?

129. What is the name of the principle river in France: The Seine or the Thames?

130. What is the name of the principle river in England: The Seine or the Thames?

131. What is the name of the principle river in the United States that is 2,320 miles long and flows from Northern Minnesota to the Gulf of Mexico: the Missouri or the Mississippi?

132. What is the name for a stream or river that flows into a main river or lake, like those found at the Colorado River and the Mississippi River: a delta or a tributary?

133. Does the Mississippi River have several tributaries or deltas?

134. What is the term for a landform that forms at the mouth of a river, where the river flows into an ocean or sea, like the one found on the Nile River: tributary or delta?

135. What is the name of the continent that you live on?

136. How many of the seven continents can you name?

137. Which continent has the highest population in the world: North America, Asia, or Africa?

138. Which country in Asia has the largest population?

139. Which continent has the lowest population in the world: Australia, Antarctica, or Asia?

140. On which continent do Spaniards, French, Italians, and Germans live: Europe or Asia?

141. In which area of Europe do Danes, Swedes, and Norwegians live: Scandinavia or the British Isles?

142. In which area of Europe do Irish, Scottish, and English live: Scandinavia or the British Isles?

143. On which continent do Egyptians, Nigerians, and Moroccans live: Africa or Asia?

144. On which continent do Chinese, Japanese, and Koreans live: Africa or Asia?

145. On which continent do Peruvians, Argentineans, and Chileans live: North America or South America?

146. What is Canada divided into: states or provinces?

147. Which continent is Canada part of: North America or Asia?

148. What are the two languages that are spoken in Canada?

149. What is Mexico divided into: states or provinces?

150. Which continent is Mexico part of: North America or South America?

151. What language is spoken in Mexico?

152. How many states is the continental United States divided into: 48 or 50?

153. Which two states are located *outside* the continental United States?

154. Which state is the **"Aloha"** state known for volcanoes, palm trees, Waikiki Beach, the Pearl Harbor Memorial, hibiscus flowers, pineapples, floral leis, grass skirts, luau parties, coconuts, sugar cane, has Honolulu as its capital, and was the last state to join the Union?

155. Which state is considered the **"Land of the Midnight Sun,"** is known for the Klondike Gold Rush, Eskimos, polar bears, forestry, wildlife, game fish, wooly mammoth fossils, husky dogs, sled-dog racing, the Northern Lights, glaciers, an oil pipeline, Mount McKinley, has Juneau as its capital, and was the 49th state to join the Union?

156. Which state is the **"Grand Canyon"** state, known for Native Americans, deserts, the Saguaro cactus flower, copper mines, the Petrified Forest, Hoover Dam, London Bridge, the Painted Desert, Fort Apache, the gunfight at the O.K. Corral, has Phoenix as its capital, and was the 48th state to join the Union?

157. Which state is called the **"Land of Enchantment,"** is known for the Carlsbad Caverns, mining, roadrunners, adobe buildings, Navajo and Apache tribes, hot air balloons, the yucca flower, the Gila National Forest, turquoise, has Santa Fe, the oldest capital city in North America as its capital, and was the 47th state to join the Union?

158. Which state is called the **"Sooner State,"** was bought as part of the Louisiana Purchase, is known for oil and coal, tornados, man-made lakes, farming, mistletoe, the "Five Civilized Tribes" *(Choctaw, Cherokee, Chickasaw, Creek and Seminole)*, the National Cowboy Hall of Fame, the Will Rogers Memorial, four mountain ranges including the Wichita Mountains, has Oklahoma City as its capital, and was the 46th state to join the Union?

159. Which state is the **"Beehive State,"** is known for its mountains, skiing, prehistoric caves and ruins, rock formations, Dinosaur National Monument, mining and farming, Mormons, lilies, seagulls, Rainbow Bridge, Great Salt Lake, has Salt Lake City as its capital, and was the 45th state to join the Union?

160. Which state is called the **"Cowboy State"** or the *"Equality State"* because it gave women the opportunity to vote in 1869, is known for sheep, cattle, bison, coal, oil, rodeos, cowboys, dude ranches, Yellowstone and Grand Teton National Parks, Old Faithful Geyser, Jackson Hole, Devil's Tower, Flaming Gorge, has Cheyenne as its capital, and was the 44th state to join the Union?

161. Which state is called the **"Panhandle State,"** is known for potatoes, elk, mining, the Shoshone Falls, Craters of the Moon National Monument, Hells Canyon, Sun Valley Ski Resort, the Appaloosa horse, has Boise as its capital, and was the 43rd state to join the Union?

162. Which state is called the **"Evergreen State,"** is known for its rain forests, apples, farming and lumber, the ferry system, rhododendron flowers, orca mammals, Mount Rainier, Mount Saint Helens, the Space Needle, the Boeing Aircraft Company, has Olympia as its capital, and was the 42nd state to join the Union?

163. Which state is called the **"Treasure State"** and is also nicknamed *"Big Sky Country,"* is known for hunting, grizzly bears, mountain goats, fresh water springs, mining for gold, silver, agate, and sapphire and oil, the Rocky Mountains, forestry, cattle, sheep farming, Ponderosa pines, Custer's Last Stand at Little Bighorn, Glacier National Park, has Helena as its capital, and was the 41st state to join the Union?

164. Which state is called the **"Coyote State,"** is known for the Black Hills, Black Hills Gold, Homestake Gold Mine, the Badlands, Wounded Knee, Mount Rushmore, wooly mammoth bones, prairie dogs, bison, has Pierre as its capital, and was the 40th state to join the Union?

165. Which state is called the "**Peace Garden State,**" is known for wheat, sunflowers, farming, Theodore Roosevelt State Park, rodeos, the Sioux Indians, has Bismarck as its capital, and was the 39th state to join the Union?

166. Which state is called the **"Centennial State,"** is known for Native Americans, bighorn sheep, skiing, aquamarines, Rocky Mountain National Park, Great Sand Dunes, the Grand Mesa flattop mountain, Pike's Peak, the Mesa Verde Ancestral Pueblo, the highest paved road in North America, the world's largest rodeo, has Denver, the mile-high city of Denver as its capital, and was the 38th state to join the Union?

167. Which state is called the **"Cornhusker State,"** is known for underwater water reserves, mammoth fossils, cottonwood trees, Chimney Rock, Agate Fossil beds, the Lewis and Clark Trail, has Lincoln as its capital, and was the 37th state to join the Union?

168. Which state is called the **"Silver State,"** is known for its gambling magnets Las Vegas, Lake Tahoe, and Reno, gold and silver mining, the Comstock Lode Silver Deposits, sagebrush, wild mustangs, the Sierra Nevada Mountain Range, Hoover Dam, has Carson City as its capital, and was the 36th state to join the Union?

169. Which state is called the **"Mountain State,"** is known for black bears, timber and coal mining, folk music, fine glass, forests, the Golden Delicious apple, Greenbrier Resort, Harper's Ferry, the Cass Scenic Railroad, has Charleston as its capital, and was the 35th state to join the Union?

170. Which state is called the **"Sunshine State,"** is known for **"amber waves of grain"** *(wheat)* production, sunflowers, cattle, dust-bowls, plane-manufacturing, was the home of Dorothy in *"The Wizard of Oz,"* has Topeka as its capital, and was the 34th state to join the Union?

171. Which state is called the **"Beaver State,"** is known for timber and lumber, grape flowers, thunder-egg geodes, Sea Lion Caves, Mount Hood Volcano, The Carousal Museum, ghost towns, Crater Lake, the deepest lake in the United States, the Columbia River, Tillamook Cheese Factory, the largest cheese factory in the world, has Salem as its capital, and was the 33rd state to join the Union?

172. Which state is called the **"Gopher State"** or the **"North Star State,"** is known as the *"land of 10,000 lakes,"* boating, The Mall of America," lady's slipper orchids, loons, Green Giant vegetables, skyways, Tonka Trucks, has St. Paul as its capital, and was the 32nd state to join the Union?

173. Which state is called the **"Golden State"** is known for redwood and giant sequoia trees, poppy flowers, the Gold Rush, Death Valley desert, rodeos, wine, oranges, cheese, raisons, turkeys, Disneyland, Spanish missions, The Golden Gate Bridge, The Pacific Coast Highway, the movie industry, has Sacramento as its capital, and was the 31st state to join the Union?

174. Which state is called the **"Badger State,"** is known for dairy, cows, fishing, 14,000 lakes, Summerfest Music Festival, robins, deer, cheese, cranberries, Muskellunge, snowmobiling, Harley Davidson motorcycles, the American Birkebeiner cross-country ski race, Noah's Ark Water Park, the Ringling Brothers Circus, the House on the Rock, the very first kindergarten, has Madison as its capital, and was the 30th state to join the Union?

175. Which state is called the "**Hawkeye State**," is known for agriculture, corn, roses, Buffalo Bill, Quaker Oats, Nordic Fest, Effigy Mounds National Monument, Winnebago Motor Homes, has Des Moines as its capital, and was the 29th state to join the Union?

176. Which state is called the "**Lone Star**" state, is known for The Alamo, Davy Crockett, oil, cotton, cattle farming, sheep farming, pecan trees, rodeos, cowboys, the Space Center, Dell Computers, the first hamburger, President Kennedy's assassination, has Austin as its capital, and was the 28th state to join the Union?

177. Which state is called the "**Sunshine**" state, is known for oranges, grapefruit, beaches, the Everglades, the Kennedy Space Center, Disney World, Epcot Center, Sea World, Cypress Gardens, Universal Studios, the Daytona 500 auto race, Gatorade, crocodiles, pumas, the "Keys," has Tallahassee as its capital, and was the 27th state to join the Union?

178. Which state is called the "**Wolverine**" state, is known for having two peninsulas, Mackinac Bridge, automobiles, Ford Motor Company, the Great Lakes, Sault St. Marie Canal, boating, navy beans, Kellogg Cereal, Petoskey Coral Stones, lighthouses, ginger ale, the world's largest weather vane, has Lansing as its capital, and was the 26th state to join the Union?

179. Which state is called the "**Land of Opportunity**," is famous for its Diamond Mine, Hot Springs National Park, the Ozarks, explorer Hernando de Soto, Crater of Diamonds State Park, the first Wal-Mart, quartz crystal, spinach, duck-calling competitions, apple blossoms, has Little Rock as its capital, and was the 25th state to join the Union?

180. Which state is called the **"Show-Me"** state, is known for the St. Louis Gateway Arch, Branson Country Music Shows, Bass Pro Shops, the Pony Express mail service, lead production, the Anheuser-Busch brewery, the first ice cream cones, Aunt Jemima pancake flour, Dr. Pepper, barbecue sauce, Mark Twain, caves, the Ozarks, has Jefferson City as its capital, and was the 24th state to join the Union?

181. Which state is called the **"Pine Tree"** state, is known for lighthouses, lobsters, sardines, blueberries, sawmills, papermaking, moose, tourmaline stones, Acadia National Park, has Augusta as its capital, and was the 23rd state to join the Union?

182. Which state is called the **"Yellowhammer"** state, is known for wild turkeys, cotton, timber, peanuts, Talladega National Forest, the Confederacy, Rosa Parks and the Montgomery Bus Boycott, the beginning of the Civil Rights Movement, the Racking Horse, cast-iron production, rocket production, the world's first electric trolley system, Gulf Coast beaches, has Montgomery as its capital, and was the 22nd state to join the Union?

183. Which state is called the **"Prairie"** state or the *"land of Lincoln,"* is known for the Willis Tower skyscraper, John Deere machinery, the tallest man in the world (8'11"), the Dairy Queen franchise, the Windy City, the Chicago Fire, Wrigley Field, Wrigley gum, Navy Pier, The Art Institute, The Chicago Theatre, The Museum of Science and Industry, the "magnificent mile" Michigan Avenue, corn, pigs, has Springfield as its capital, and was the 21st state to join the Union?

184. Which state is called the **"Magnolia"** state, is known for its southern magnolia trees, river boats, "Old Man River," the largest river in the United States, Theodore Roosevelt's "Teddy Bear," catfish, cotton, tree farms, "Blues" music, Pine-

Sol cleaner, the first 4-H club, the International Checkers Hall of Fame, Coca-Cola, has Jackson as its capital, and was the 20th state to join the Union?

185. Which state is called the **"Hoosier"** state, is known for the Indianapolis 500 auto race, corn, the first gasoline pump, basketball, the "Brain Bank of the Midwest" with many colleges and universities located there, the first Raggedy Ann Doll, interstate highways, the Saturday Evening Post, has Indianapolis as its capital, and was the 19th state to join the Union?

186. Which state is called the **"Pelican"** state, is known for pelicans, Breaux Bridge, the "crawfish capital of the world," farming, frogs, alligators, tall cypress trees, Mardi Gras in New Orleans, the French quarter, jazz, the first Tarzan movie, the Superdome, Cajun descendants, "parishes" instead of counties, has Baton Rouge as its capital, and was the 18th state to join the Union?

187. Which state is called the **"Buckeye"** state, is known for its buckeye trees, farming, the Pro Football Hall of Fame, the Rock and Roll Hall of Fame, rubber and bicycle tires, greenhouse plants, the first chewing gum, first cash register, first professional baseball team, first traffic light, first airplane by the Wright brothers, first police, fire, and ambulance service, has Columbus as its capital, and was the 17th state to join the Union?

188. Which state is called the **"Volunteer"** state, is known for the Grand Ole Opry, Elvis's former home Graceland, Great Smoky Mountains National Park, the Country Music Hall of Fame, Bluegrass music, horses, salamanders, turtles, aluminum, zinc, caves, whitewater rafting, has Nashville as its capital, and was the 16th state to join the Union?

189. Which state is called the **"Bluegrass"** state, is known for the blue grasses on the prairie, covered bridges, tobacco, whiskey, pickles, a horse derby, Mammoth Cave National Park, the long rifle, the largest amount of gold stored in the world, the Chevrolet Corvette, the first Mother's Day, has Frankfort as its capital, and was the 15th state to join the Union?

190. Which state is called the **"Green Mountain"** state, is known for ski resorts, autumn colors, Morgan horses, maple syrup, Ethan Allan and his revolutionary Green Mountain Boys, dairy farming, granite and marble mines, the first Ben and Jerry's Ice Cream Store, having the lowest crime rate in the nation, the Von Trapp Family of Austria made famous in the musical *"The Sound of Music,"* the Bing Cosby Christmas classic, *"White Christmas,"* has Montpelier as its capital, and was the 14th state to join the Union?

191. Which state is called the **"Ocean"** state, is known for red chickens, red maple trees, Newport's summer tourism, the first circus, Arkwright's *"Spinning Jenny,"* cotton mills, textiles and electronics, silverware and jewelry, the Tennis Hall of Fame, the first National Lawn Tennis Tournament, the oldest school house in the United States, The Flying Horse Carousal, being the smallest state in the nation, has Providence as its capital, and was the 13th state to join the Union?

192. Which state is called the **"Tar Heel"** or *"Old North"* state, is known for being the "barbecue capital of the world," the Cherokee Native Americans, Great Smokey Mountains National Park, Whitewater Falls, Pepsi, Krispy Kreme doughnuts, the Venus Fly- Trap, sweet potatoes, emeralds, furniture-making, tobacco and brick production, the first miniature golf course, Biltmore Estate, the nation's largest home, the Wright Brothers as the "First in Flight" at Kitty

Hawk, has Raleigh as its capital and was the 12th state to join the Union?

193. Which state is called the **"Empire"** state, is known for Niagara Falls, the Catskill Mountains, the Adirondack Mountains, Long Island, Ellis Island, Staten Island and the Staten Island Ferry, Coney Island and the Coney Island Cyclone rollercoaster, Manhattan, Queens, the Bronx, the Bronx Zoo, Yonkers, Brooklyn, the Brooklyn Bridge, the Erie Canal, orchids, dairy farming, jazz, Yankee Stadium, Babe Ruth, The Statue of Liberty, Central Park, Radio City Music Hall, The Apollo Theatre, Times Square, Radio City Music Hall and the Rockettes, Madison Square Garden, Rockefeller Center, Lincoln Center, Broadway, The Empire State Building, The Metropolitan Museum of Art, The Museum of Modern Art, Saks 5th Avenue, Macy's Thanksgiving Day Parade, Tiffany's jewelry store, St. Paul's Cathedral, The Baseball Hall of Fame, The United Nations, , the stock exchange, the first license plates, the first toilet paper, marshmallows, Jell-O, the first pizzeria, the longest running newspaper, the nation's largest public library, subways, being the most populated city in the nation, has Albany as its capital, and was the 11th state to join the Union?

194. Which state is called the **"Old Dominion,"** is known as the ***"birthplace of a nation"*** as well as for the first Colonial settlement at Jamestown, was the site of thousands of Civil War battles, the state of surrenders from both the Revolutionary and the Civil Wars, the site of Patrick Henry's speech, *"Give Me Liberty or Give Me Death,"* home of the Blue Ridge Mountains, oysters, tobacco, the first peanuts, ship-building, Robert E. Lee, Arlington National Cemetery, the tomb of the Unknown Soldier, Chesapeake Bay Bridge Tunnel, the Pentagon, NATO headquarters, Thomas Jefferson's home Monticello, George Washington's home

Mount Vernon, has Richmond as its capital, and was the 10th state to join the Union?

195. Which state is called the **"Granite"** state, is known for its autumn colors, logging, leather work, farming, White Mountain National Forest, maple syrup, the first public library, the oldest pipe organ, the center for covered wagon-building, the longest covered bridge crossing 460 feet over the Connecticut River, is the home of the Clydesdales horses, poet Robert Frost, the first alarm clock, has Concord as its capital, and was the 9th state to join the Union?

196. Which state is called the **"Palmetto"** state, is known for being the first state to break away from the Union at Fort Sumter, palmetto trees, the Blue Ridge Mountains, tobacco, peaches, ginkgo farms, furniture-making, basket-making, Myrtle Beach, Hilton Head Resorts, golf courses, the Thoroughbred Racing Hall of Fame, has Columbia as its capital, and was the 8th state to join the Union?

197. Which state is called the **"Old Line"** state, is known for the Annapolis U.S. Naval Academy, shipping, Chesapeake Bay oysters, crabs, tobacco, John Hopkins University, the first school, the first refrigerator, the Mason-Dixon Line marking the boundary between this state and Pennsylvania, the first telegraph, wild ponies, sailing, Baltimore Oriole birds, has Annapolis as its capital, and was the 7th state to join the Union?

198. Which state is called the **"Old Colony"** state, is known for the Pilgrims' arrival on the Mayflower at Plymouth, the first Thanksgiving with the Native Americans, the Revolutionary War battles at Lexington, Concord, and Bunker Hill, Boston Harbor, the Boston Tea Party, the Freedom Trail, Beacon Hill, the Old North Church, Paul Revere's House, Copley Square, Faneuil Hall, Bunker Hill Monument, the Old State House and the first reading of the Declaration of Independence, the

Boston Pops, the Charles River Esplanade, Cape Cod, Nantucket Island, Martha's Vineyard, the first college now called Harvard University, the Boston Terrier, Boston baked beans, Boston Cream Pie, clam chowder, cranberries, the first Toll House chocolate chip cookies, the first Dunkin Donuts, Johnny Appleseed, Fenway Park, the John F. Kennedy Library, the John Hancock building, has Boston as its capital, and was the 6th state to join the Union?

199. Which state is called the **"Constitution"** state, is known for providing goods to George Washington's Continental Army during the Revolution, the inventions of Eli Whitney's cotton gin, Charles Goodyear's tire, Linus Yale's lock, Yale University, the first law school, nuclear submarine production, the first telephone book, cattle and pig branding, the first color television, the first Polaroid Camera, the first car insurance, has Hartford as its capital, and was the 5th state to join the Union?

200. Which state is called the **"Peach"** state, is known for the production of peanuts, cotton, and peaches, chickens, the Okefenokee Swamps, the Masters Golf Tournament in Augusta, Stone Mountain Park, the carvings of Stonewall Jackson, Jefferson Davis, and Robert E. Lee on the side of Stone Mountain making it the largest granite sculpture in the world, the Blue Ridge Scenic Railway, Ante-Bellum pre-war houses, was the location for the classic move, *"Gone With the Wind,"* has Atlanta as its capital, and was the 4th state to join the Union?

201. Which state is called the **"Garden"** state, is known for its garden vegetables, horses, the longest boardwalk in the world, seaside resorts, casinos, Princeton University, the chemical industry, shopping malls, the "Miss America" pageant, the first Indian Reservation, Edison's inventions of the light bulb, movie projector, and phonograph, the first

drive-in movie theatre, has its cities featured on the "Monopoly" board game, is home to "Lucy the Elephant" six-story building, is the most densely populated state, is almost completely surrounded by water, has Trenton as its capital, and was the third state to join the Union?

202. Which state is called the **"Keystone"** state, is known for its Quaker founder William Penn, Independence Hall, the signing of the Declaration of Independence, the writing of the United States Constitution, the Liberty Bell, first American flag, Gettysburg, Valley Forge, farming, coal production, steel production, mushroom production, Hershey's chocolate, Christmas trees, the first public zoo, the world's first oil well, the first piano, the first computer, a high concentration of Amish, has Harrisburg as its capital, and was the 2nd state to join the Union?

203. Which state is called the **"First"** state, is known for being the first state to ratify the U.S. Constitution, the Chesapeake and Delaware canal, chemical production, chicken farming, the blue hen chicken, ladybugs, horseshoe crabs, nylon production, processed foods, historic churches, Finnish log cabins, has Dover as its capital, and was the 1st state to join the Union?

204. What is the **largest** state in the continental United States after Alaska?

205. What is the **smallest** state in the continental United States?

206. What is the capital of the United States?

207. What do the letters **"D.C."** stand for as part of our capital's name?

208. Which ocean borders the United States on the eastern coast: the Atlantic or the Pacific?

209. Which ocean borders the United States on the western coast: the Atlantic or the Pacific?

210. What is the name of the country that borders America to the North?

211. What is the name of the country that borders America to the South?

212. What are the other states that border the state you live in?

213. Can you name any of the **counties** (or *parishes* if you live in Louisiana) that border the county *(parish)* you live in?

214. Does the United States of America have symbols that represent it?

215. What national symbol has red and white stripes, and fifty white stars on a blue background?

216. How many stripes are there on the American Flag, representing the number of original colonies that declared independence from Great Britain and became the first states in the Union?

217. What national oath do U.S. citizens recite while facing the flag that shows their loyalty to the United States?

218. What is the name of the lady that is credited with making one of the original American flags: Betsy Ross or Martha Washington?

219. What is the name of the American symbol located in Independence Hall in Philadelphia, Pennsylvania that cracked soon after it was rung?

220. What is the national bird of the United States: the bald eagle or the hawk?

221. What is the name of the American symbol located in New York Harbor on Liberty Island that was a gift from France, and depicts a lady holding a torch high above her head?

222. What American national symbol is a document proclaiming the independence of the thirteen original colonies from Great Britain?

223. What American document was approved at a Convention in Philadelphia in 1787, includes the Bill of Rights and several amendments, and is considered the supreme law of the land?

224. What is the name of the *patriotic song* that was based on a poem written by Francis Scott King during the War of 1812, was adopted by Congress in 1931, and is the official national song of the United States: God Bless America or The Star-Spangled Banner?

225. What kind of symbols do states have that represent that state?

226. What American landmark located in South Dakota has four American presidents carved in into a mountain: Mount Rushmore or Mount Blanc?

227. Who is the fourth president, besides Washington, Jefferson, and Lincoln that is carved into the granite face at Mount Rushmore: Adams or Roosevelt?

228. Are the following national monuments and memorials located in Washington D.C. or Virginia: Lincoln Memorial, Jefferson Monument, National Mall, Washington Monument, World War II Memorial, Vietnam Veterans Memorial, Korean War Veterans Memorial, FDR Memorial, the Capitol Building, and the White House?

229. What is the name of the memorial located at 1600 Pennsylvania Avenue in Washington D.C?

230. Are the following national monuments and memorials located in Washington D.C. or Virginia: Arlington National Cemetery, Washington's home Mount Vernon, Jefferson's home Monticello, Booker T. Washington Memorial, Pentagon Memorial, and Iwo Jima Memorial?

231. What is the name of the memorial located in the National Mall that is the world's tallest stone obelisk towering 555 feet high: The Washington Monument or The Space Needle?

232. What is another name for the memorial U.S. Marine Corps War Memorial in Virginia that honors the marines that defended America during World War in a battle with the Japanese, and is a statue of four marines raising the American flag: Hiroshima or Iwo Jima?

233. What is the name for the international landmark that is the collective name for three *waterfalls* called Horseshoe, American, and Bridal Veil that border the Canadian province of Ontario and the state of New York: Niagara Falls or Yosemite Falls?

234. What kind of American landmark are all of the following: Rocky Mountain, Mammoth Cave, Glacier, Crater Lake, Yosemite, Badlands, Great Smokey Mountains, Everglades, Acadia, Death Valley, Grand Teton, Yellowstone, Hot Springs, Mesa Verde, and Redwood?

235. What landmarks or monuments can you name in your state?

236. Can history be divided into different periods?

237. Did the Stone Age, Bronze Age, and Iron Age occur in ancient history or modern history?

238. Does the civilization of Mesopotamia in the region in Southeast Asia fall under prehistory or modern history?

239. Which country is referred to as the *"cradle of civilization:"* China or Mesopotamia?

240. What is the name of the current country where *Mesopotamia* once was: Iraq or India?

241. What ancient civilization translates in Greek as, **"Land between the Rivers:"** Mesopotamia or Egypt?

242. What are the names of the rivers located in Mesopotamia: the Tigris and Euphrates, or the Nile and Danube?

243. What type of societal system did Mesopotamia have: a class system or an estate system?

244. What was the name of the ancient capital of the country of **Babylonia,** located along the banks of the Euphrates River in Mesopotamia: Babylon or Baghdad?

245. What is the name of the ruler of Babylon, considered the greatest ruler of the first Babylonian dynasty, credited for developing a Code of Laws: Hammurabi or Herod?

246. Which civilization was the first to develop the entity of the city, writing, government, the calendar, glass, the wheel, the potter's wheel, the aqueduct, astronomy, the 60-minute hour, the sundial, irrigation systems, and agriculture: Greece or Mesopotamia?

247. Were Mesopotamians known for developing agriculture, government, religion, and city-states?

248. What is the term for the first **writing system** of the Mesopotamian using a chisel and a clay tablet: cuneiform or hieroglyphics?

249. Where did the empires of Sumerian, Babylonian, and Assyrian exist: Greece or Mesopotamia?

250. What was the name for the earliest inhabitants of Mesopotamia: the Babylonians or the Sumerians?

251. What was the name for the last race of Mesopotamia, and the first to develop iron weapons and use chariots: the Babylonians or the Assyrians?

252. What is the name of the earliest inhabitants of Mesopotamia that invented the wheel: the Sumerians or the Assyrians??

253. What farming machine was first invented in Mesopotamia: the seed plow or the tractor?

254. What number did the Mesopotamians use to calculate the minutes in an hour that was based on astronomy and the moon: 24 or 60?

255. What is the name for the sacred Sumerian structures built to honor the main god of the city, were the highest structures in the area, and resembled a step pyramid: ziggurats or temples?

256. What is the name of one of the *Ancient Wonders of the World* located in Babylon: The Great Pyramid or The Hanging Gardens?

257. What is the name given for the historical time period between Ancient and Modern: The Early Modern Era or The Middle Ages?

258. What is the name given for the time that is associated with castles, knights, armor, King Arthur, and Joan of Arc that began after the fall of the Western Roman Empire: renaissance or medieval?

259. What is the name for the last major group in the *feudal system* of people during medieval times after the king, the bishops, the barons, and the lords: the commoners or the peasants?

260. What is the term that refers to the medieval *farmer* who worked the land for his lord and paid him dues in exchange for the use of the land: peasant or serf?

261. What is the name given to the people that took control over the Western Roman Empire after Germanic tribes ruled it for a short time: The Barbarians or the Greeks?

262. What is another name for the Eastern Roman Empire that included Greece, Turkey, and the Middle East: Byzantine or Barbarian?

263. What was the name of the capital of the Eastern Roman Empire: Constantinople or Istanbul?

264. Who were the nomadic herdsmen from *Mongolia*, a country north of China that destroyed much of Europe and Asia between the 3rd and 5th centuries: the Visigoths or the Huns?

265. What is the name for the most successful king of the **Huns**: Herod or Attila?

266. What is the name for what is attached to the bottom of a horse saddle that gave the Huns an advantage when fighting on horseback with their enemies: reins or stirrups?

267. What is the name for the group of Germanic people regarded as *Barbarians* that are most known for conquering Rome with destruction and looting: The Vandals or the Visigoths?

268. What is the name for the nomadic tribe who took most of southern France from the Romans but were later forced out by the German Franks, and eventually settled in Spain: the Huns or the Visigoths?

269. What is the name of the group that England is named for that took over Britain in the Middle Ages: the Angles or the Jutes?

270. What is the name of the group of people who merged with the Angles in Britain that the Old English language originated from: the Visigoths or the Saxons?

271. What is the term that was created by an Italian poet that refers to the Middle Ages after the fall of the Western Roman Empire, characterized by intellectual darkness, social chaos, warfare, and poverty: Medieval Times or Dark Ages?

272. What is the name of the official religion of the Roman Empire that experienced significant growth during the Middle Ages: Judaism or Christianity?

273. What is the name of the leader of the Christian church in Rome: The Pope or the Bishop?

274. What is the other main religion besides Roman Catholicism that was formed in the Middle Ages: Orthodoxy or Judaism?

275. What is the name for the men who devoted their lives to the church in the Middle Ages and lived in *monasteries*: monks or friars?

276. What is the name for the women who devoted their lives to the church in the Middle Ages and studied the writings of the ancient Romans and Greeks: abbesses or nuns?

277. Who was the *King of the Franks* of Germany, expanded the Frankish Empire, and was also a former Roman Emperor whose name means *"Charles the Great:"* Charlemagne or Carlos?

278. What is the term given for the legal and social system in medieval times in which service was exchanged for land: feudalism or serfdom?

279. What were the three major groups of people during medieval times: nobility, church, and commoners, or lords, ladies, and serfs?

280. Who was more powerful: the lord or the king?

281. Who was the person that received a piece of land, acted as a servant, and promised loyalty to the lord: the serf or the vassal?

282. Who was the person that *owned* the land in a feudal system: the lord or the vassal?

283. What was the term used for the land grant contract that a lord provided to a vassal: a contract or a fief?

284. Could vassals promise their loyalty to more than one lord?

285. What is the medieval term for *fighters* supplied to the king by the lord: warriors or knights?

286. What is the name of the *lowest* member of a feudal class that performed labor on the farms and manors owned by a lord: a serf or a knight?

287. What is the name of the medieval stone structure where the lords and kings lived that provided protection from raids and attacks: a labyrinth or a castle?

288. What is the medieval term for a traveling musician that entertained the children: a jester or a minstrel?

289. What is the medieval term for a clown that entertained the children: a jester or a minstrel?

290. What is the name of a game played on the lawn that many adults and children played during the Middle Ages: croquet or lacrosse?

291. What is the medieval term for a young boy who did simple things like waiting on tables for noblemen and knights: a page or a servant?

292. What could a medieval page become after *seven* years of faithful service to a nobleman, and was considered a trainee to a knight: a squire or a page?

293. What is the name of the poem about a squire written by the English poet **Geoffrey Chaucer** during the Middle Ages: "The Canterbury Tales," or "Knights at the Roundtable?"

294. Who might have a horse, weapons, and armor: a knight or a squire?

295. Could Noble girls train to be knights, or were they typically trained to sew, weave, and spin?

296. What is the medieval term for battles on horseback using lances: bullfighting or jousting?

297. What is the medieval term for the *code of conduct* of a knight that included bravery, courtesy, and honor: chivalry or loyalty?

298. Did many medieval towns have craftsmen, farmers, and traders?

299. Did merchants and craftsmen hold power in medieval towns?

300. What is the term for the association of medieval craftsmen that regulated prices and trace: a union or a guild?

301. What is the term for a person that is learning a new trade: a master or an apprentice?

302. What could an apprentice be promoted to after working for a master at least seven years: a master or a journeyman?

303. What could a journeyman be promoted to after learning the trade at an expert level: an apprentice or a master?

304. Was **religion** important in medieval days?

305. Did medieval England become stronger when the Angles and the Saxons united under King Edward the Confessor and converted to Christianity?

306. Was Normandy, France under Duke William a weak or a strong kingdom?

307. Where did Duke William travel to in 1066 with several hundred ships and thousands of Knights in order to defeat and conquer King Harold and his Anglo-Saxon army: England or Spain?

308. What was the other name of the newly crowned King William I: William the Conqueror or William the Great?

309. Did the Anglo-Saxons object when King William promoted his Norman knights to English noblemen, built castles in England, and collected taxes from them?

310. What is the name of the person who became the King of England after the death of William the Conqueror: William II or Henry I?

311. Did King Henry I and King Henry II inherit the throne after William II?

312. Did Henry II establish a strong government and new law system that is the basis of court procedures as we know them today?

313. Is King Henry II credited for establishing **English Common Law**?

314. Did King John, King Henry's son, add to England's kingdom, or did he manage to give up much of England's land to France?

315. Who were the wealthy people of England that had to give up some of their power to King John and pay more in taxes:

counts, dukes, lords, and earls, or peasants, journeymen, serfs, and knights?

316. What is the name of the *document* that was created initially in 1215 to limit the rights of King John, guaranteed the rights of the average citizen from the King of England, and helped lay the groundwork for English Common Law and, later, the U.S. Constitution: the Magna Carta, the Declaration of Independence, or The Bill or Rights?

317. What did King John's grandson Edward I create to make the royal government stronger, consisting of knights and nobles who approved the laws of the king: a Parliament or an Assembly?

318. What was the name given for the mysterious disease, now known as the *Bubonic plague,* that killed millions of people in Europe in the 1300's and showed up as dark patches on the skin: Yellow Fever, Black Death, or Measles?

319. What is the name for the string of conflicts in France between the armies of the kings of France and England that lasted between 1337 and 1453, and ended when King Edward's son *"The Black Prince,"* captured King John II of France: The Hundred Years' War or The French and English War?

320. What is the name of the **peasant girl** from medieval France who felt that she had a calling, led a French army to several victories during *The Hundred Years War*, forced the English out of Orleans, and was burned at the stake at the age of nineteen: Joan of Arc or Lady Antoinette?

321. Do many people consider the end of the Middle Ages in 1453 the same as the end of The Hundred Years War?

322. What major *empire* ended in 1453 after Turkish invaders captured the capital of Constantinople: the Byzantine Empire or the Ottoman Empire?

323. What are Christianity, Judaism, Buddhism, and Islam all regarded as: world races or world religions?

324. What is the name of the religion that is practiced by over one billion Muslims, believing that there is one God, and that Mohammad is the prophet: Islam or Buddhism?

325. What is the name of the holiest place in Saudi Arabia where Muslims believe that Mohammad received the word of God whom they call Allah, and is the pilgrimage for all Islam believers: Fatima or Mecca?

326. What is the name for the shrine and the most sacred site in Mecca where Muslims go to pray: Kaaba or Quran?

327. What is the name of the first domed shrine to be built in Jerusalem, Israel where Mohammad is said to have begun his rise to Heaven from the top of a rock: Dome of the Rock or The Great Mosque?

328. What is the name of the city that Mohammad and his followers moved to after being forced out of Mecca due to conflicts with traders: Medina or Jerusalem?

329. What is the Islamic name for the journey of Mohammad and his followers from Mecca to Medina that also marks the beginning of the Muslim calendar: Hijra or Quran?

330. What is the general term for the Muslim place of worship that has towers from which worshippers are led in prayer five times a day: a Temple or a Mosque?

331. What is the name of the Mosque in Mecca: The Grand Mosque or the Mosque of the Prophet?

332. What is the name of the Mosque in Medina: The Grand Mosque or The Prophet's Mosque?

333. What is the Islamic term for a Muslim war waged by those in defense of the Islamic faith, like that led by Mohammad against non-believers in Mecca: Hijra of Jihad?

334. What is the name of the *holy book* of the Islamic religion written in Arabic that Muslims believe to be the word of God: the Quran or the Makkah?

335. What is the term for the **five rules** that represent the five primary obligations of Muslims that include a profession of faith, prayer, giving alms to the poor, fasting during the holy month of Ramadan, and a pilgrimage to Mecca: The Five Islamic Rules or The Five Pillars of Islam?

336. Did the Muslims conquer other places in the Middle East, Africa, and Spain after the death of Mohammad in order to spread the Islam religion?

337. Did the Muslims live in Spain and build many mosques and palaces there?

338. What is the name of the **Moorish palace** located in Granada, Spain and named for King Alhamar with its renowned *Court of the Lions,* and is regarded as an elaborate example of Arabic architecture: the Alcázar or the Alhambra?

339. What is the name of the southern **Spanish city** that become a center of Muslim culture and further study of the Quran: Sevilla or Córdoba?

340. Do Muslims consider Jerusalem a holy city?

341. What was the name of the military conflicts between European Christians in the 11th, 12th, and 13th centuries who wanted to win back Jerusalem *(the Holy Land)* from the Muslims: the Crusades or the Holy Wars?

342. What is the term for the **numbers** like 1, 2, and 3 that were first introduced by the Muslims and then taught these symbols to Europeans: Roman numerals or Arabic numerals?

343. What is the name of the people of both Arab and Berber descent from northern Africa that occupied Spain and Portugal for several hundred years: the Moors or the Moroccans?

344. What is the **second** largest continent in the world: Asia or Africa?

345. What is the name of the largest desert in the world in northern Africa: Sahara or Kalahari?

346. What is the name of the mountain range in northern Africa: Atlas or Pyrenees?

347. What is the geographical term for a *flat* area of grass in a tropical region with tall grasses and only a few trees that is the habitat for many African animals: woodlands or savanna?

348. What is the name of the world's deepest river located in Africa that is a big economic resource for the continent, and provides parts of Africa with hydroelectric power: the Nile or the Congo?

349. On which continent are Egypt, Ethiopia, Nigeria, and Morocco located?

350. Which country in Africa is known for its pyramids, tombs, and kings: Egypt or Morocco?

351. What name did Egyptians use for *king* meaning supreme ruler: Pharaoh or Chariot?

352. Did the ancient Egyptians regard the Pharaoh as a God?

353. Did Pharaohs have a hierarchy of rulers under them?

354. Were the wives of the Pharaohs second or third in power?

355. What is the term for the *leader* of the Egyptian government: the Vizier or the Monarch?

356. Did citizens pay taxes to support the government?

357. What is the term for the period of rule when Kings or Pharaohs come from the same family for several generations: dynasty or regime?

358. Was Egypt ruled by several dynasties?

359. Was ancient Egypt divided into Upper and Lower Egypt, or Upper, Middle, and Lower Egypt?

360. What is the name of the **first pharaoh** that united Upper Egypt and Lower Egypt into one single country: King Tut or King Menes?

361. What was the capital of Egypt during the Old Kingdom era: Memphis or Thebes?

362. What was the capital of Egypt during the New Kingdom era: Memphis or Thebes?

363. What is the current capital of Egypt: Cairo or Thebes?

364. What is the name of the **Great Pyramids** that were built during the Old Kingdom: Giza or Sphinx?

365. Is the *Great Pyramid of Giza* also known as the Pyramid of Cheops or the Pyramid of Khufu?

366. Which pyramid in Egypt is the oldest and largest of three limestone pyramids that has a perfectly square base, and is the oldest of the Seven Wonders of the ancient world: the Pyramid of Teotihuacán or the Great Pyramid of Giza?

367. What is the name of one of the greatest monumental limestone sculptures in the ancient world from 2500 B.C. that has a lion's body and the head of a Pharaoh, is located near Giza, and is a national symbol of Egypt: the Great Pyramid or the Great Sphinx?

368. What was the purpose of the **Sphinx**: to honor Pharaohs or to guard the temples and tombs?

369. How long is the Great Sphinx: 240 feet long or 20 feet long?

370. What feature of the Sphinx's face has been mysteriously knocked off: the nose or the ear?

371. What is the name for the natural weathering that has affected the appearance of the Sphinx thousands of years later: erosion or sandstorms?

372. What is the name for the tall, narrow monument that the Egyptians built two of near the entrance of a sacred temple: obelisk or pillar?

373. What is the name of the Queen of Egypt, wife of King Akhenaton that reigned between 1353 and1336 B.C., played an active role in religious life, and has a symbolic painted bust of her face because of her great beauty that is now located in Berlin's Egyptian Museum: Nefertiti or Cleopatra?

374. What Egyptian Pharaoh became king at the age of 9, ruled Egypt between 1334 and 1325 B.C., and is known today primarily because of the 1922 discovery of his tomb in *The Valley of the Kings*: King Menes or King Tutankhamen?

375. What is the name of the Pharaoh that is considered the greatest Pharaoh of Ancient Egypt that ruled from 1279 B.C. to 1213 B.C, was regarded as a great military leader, and built many temples during his reign: Ramses II or Nefertiti?

376. What is the name for the image on the crown of an Egyptian headdress worn only by pharaohs: cobra goddess or python goddess?

377. Where is King Tutankhamen's tomb located in Egypt: The Valley of the Kings or The Valley of the Gods?

378. Who discovered King "Tut's" tomb with over 5,000 artifacts including gold, chariots, statues, boats, jewelry, and his golden coffin: Howard Carter or Hiram Bingham?

379. What was often found on the **walls** of tombs: paintings or carvings?

380. What was the name of the **book** that many Egyptians wanted in their tomb that was written on papyrus or on the walls of the tomb that would empower them in the after-life and offer them protection through magic spells: the Book of Life or the Book of the Dead?

381. Who has taken much of the valuable art and artifacts that had been buried inside Egyptian tombs: archeologists or vandals?

382. What is the word for the Egyptian process of preserving or embalming a pharaoh or a person of wealth by wrapping the body with many layers of linen cloth in order to prepare it for the afterlife: cremation or mummification?

383. Did the Egyptians use arithmetic, algebra, geometry, and fractions in their calculations?

384. What mathematical system did the Egyptians use to help build their pyramids and tombs, calculate time, land area, and cooking using the numbers 1, 10, and 100: the binary system or the decimal system?

385. What is the term for the system of **writing** using pictures and symbols during one of the earliest dynasties: cave drawings or hieroglyphics?

386. Did *hieroglyphics* use consonant sounds or vowel sounds?

387. What is the name for the people of Egypt that could read and write hieroglyphics after years of practice, and typically came from rich families: pages or scribes?

388. Could all ancient Egyptians read and write, or was it primarily scribes that could do this?

389. What is the name of the **stone** that was discovered in Egypt by a French soldier that had the same message written in both hieroglyphics and in Greek that made it easy to translate: the Rosetta Stone or the Blarney Stone?

390. What kind of job did most ancient Egyptians have: farmers, priests, soldiers, or craftspeople?

391. Did the Egyptians wear *make-up* both for sun protection and to make a fashion statement?

392. What accessory did many Egyptians wear around their necks made of gold, silver, or copper?

393. What were the houses of many ancient Egyptians made from: stone or mud bricks?

394. What was the staple food of many commoner Egyptians: bread or meat?

395. Who is credited for inventing locks, black ink, eye makeup, parchment paper from the papyrus plant, medicine, the ox plow, and the 365-day calendar: the Egyptians or the Ethiopians?

396. What is the name of the people that conquered Africa in 525 B.C, ruled Africa for over one hundred years, and are renowned for their handcrafted rugs: the Persians or the Babylonians?

397. What is the name for the ancient civilization *south* of Egypt known for trade and for pyramids, existing between 1000

B.C. and 300 A.D: the Kingdom of Kush or the Kingdom of Axum?

398. What is the name of the King of ancient Greece in 336 B.C, began the dynasty that ruled Africa for 300 years after he conquered Egypt and the Persian Empire, and founded the city of Alexandria: Ibn Battuta or Alexander the Great?

399. What is the name of the dynasty of 305 B.C. when **Ptolemy I** became the Pharaoh and Alexandria became the first capital: Ptolemaic or Persian?

400. What is the name of the *last* pharaoh of Egypt that ruled Egypt after the death of Alexander the Great, could speak seven languages, had romances with Romans Julius Caesar and Marc Antony, and supposedly allowed a poisonous cobra snake to bite her after she heard of the death of Marc Antony: Cleopatra or Queen Nefertiti?

401. What is the name for the **valley** in Egypt where tombs were constructed for the Pharaohs or Kings who ruled from 1500 B.C. to 1000 B.C: the Valley of the Kings or the Tombs of the Pharaohs?

402. What is the name of the **river** that flows through Egypt south to north, is the longest river in the world, is a good place for farming wheat and papyrus because of its fertile, black soil, and provides a common means for transporting goods: the Congo or the Nile?

403. What is the geographic term for the area where the Nile River splits into several branches before emptying into the Mediterranean: a delta or a tributary?

404. Does Egypt have deserts, mountains, oases, and wetlands?

405. What is the name for the **plant** grown near the Nile River that the Egyptians used to make parchment paper in order that

they could write religious texts and important documents: Eucalyptus or Papyrus?

406. What did the ancient Egyptians use to make ropes, sandals, and baskets: papyrus or straw?

407. What materials did the Egyptians build their boats with: papyrus reeds or birch bark?

408. What kind of boats did ancient Egyptians build use to navigate up and down the Nile in order to conduct trade with other countries: cargo ships or reed boats?

409. What humped animal did traders bring back from Arabia around 400 A.D. that could go several days without water, carry a big load, and had the endurance to cross the Sahara Desert?

410. What is the word for a group of **travelers** on a journey through the desert: a caravan or a convoy?

411. What did many traders from western Africa trade their ivory tusks and gold for: salt or papyrus?

412. Did the ancient Egyptians have an organized army?

413. What is the name for the wheeled **carriage** pulled by two horses that would carry two Egyptian soldiers and their bows and arrows: a caravan or a chariot?

414. What were the *Kush, Axum, Ghana, Mali,* and *Songhai* all considered: West African Empires or Egyptian Pharaohs?

415. Who is the Muslim leader of **Mali** from Morocco who wrote about his travels that included his journey to the palace in Timbuktu: Mansa Musa or Ibn Battuta?

416. What is the term for ancient African storytellers and entertainers who would tell a story a while singing, dancing, or playing the drum: gypsies or griots?

417. How many *independent* nations are located in Africa: 54 or 82?

418. Which continent is regarded as one of the most underdeveloped continents in the world?

419. What **disease** do thousands of Africans die from every year, caused by a bite from a parasite-infected mosquito: Yellow Fever or Malaria?

420. What is the estimated population of Africa: one billion or 500 million?

421. What is the name of the scientist that theorized that our ancestors came from Africa: Jonas Salk or Charles Darwin?

422. What is the biggest country in Africa: Sudan or Kenya?

423. What is the highest point in Africa located in Tanzania: Mt. McKinley or Mt. Kilimanjaro?

424. What is the name of the **cape** in South Africa on the Atlantic Ocean that explorer Vasco de Gama sailed around from Portugal in order to reach the east: Cape Cod or Cape of Good Hope?

425. What is the name of the **waterway** that was built in 1869 that connects the Mediterranean with the Red Sea and took over ten years to build: The Panama Canal or The Suez Canal?

426. What is the name of the **dam** across the Nile River completed in 1970 that has improved irrigation and agriculture in Egypt: the Niger Dam or the Aswan Dam?

427. What is the name of the *Egyptian President* that signed a peace treaty with Israel's Prime Minister Menachem Begin in 1978: Anwar Sadat or Gamal Abdel Nasser?

428. What is the name of the area in Africa that is named this because it was the primary source of **ivory** at the beginning of the 19th century: Ivory Coast or Tusk Terrain?

429. What are the two main rivers in Africa: the Nile and the Congo, or the Nile and the Niger?

430. What are the two main deserts in Africa: the Mojave and Atacama, or the Sahara and Kalahari?

431. Could the Sahara Desert fit into the borders of the United States?

432. Where do many African animals live: the Sahara or the Savanna?

433. What African animals can you name that live in the Savannas?

434. What is the largest living land animal in Africa?

435. Which animals might you see at the *zoo* that come from Africa?

436. What country in Africa is famous for its jungles, safaris, wildlife preserves, and national parks where you can see many elephants, giraffes, lions, zebras, and rhinoceros: Nigeria or Kenya?

437. Which African animal is considered the *fastest* land animal, running up to 60 miles per hour?

438. What would Arabic, Swahili, French, and Portuguese be categorized as?

439. How many different languages are spoken in Africa: 200 or 2000?

440. Do you think that many African tribes speak their own, unique language?

441. What is the most common language spoken in Africa: Arabic or French?

442. What is the most common religion in Africa: Islam or Christianity?

443. What is the name of the holiday that falls in the ninth month in the Islamic calendar, is a time of praying, fasting, and self-reflection, and is celebrated throughout the world by over one billion Muslims: Kwanzaa or Ramadan?

444. What is the biggest *island* off the coast of Africa: Madagascar or the Canary Islands?

445. What **craft** is Africa famous for: masks or puppets?

446. What kind of **musical instrument** is Africa most famous for?

447. What is the name of the *civil rights activist* that was elected President of South Africa in 1994 when the first democratic elections were held: Nelson Mandela or Muammar Gaddafi?

448. What is the term for the racist political policy in South Africa that separated people based on their skin color, forcing blacks and whites to live apart until 1993: segregation or apartheid?

449. What is the name of the divisive Libyan leader and dictator who ruled Libya for 42 years: Nelson Mandela or Muammar Gaddafi?

450. Do many Africans celebrate both Muslim and Christian holidays depending on their beliefs?

451. What is the name for the weeklong reflective holiday here in the United States that honors and celebrates African heritage and history: African Week or Kwanzaa?

452. What is the name of the Disney movie and Broadway musical, based on an imaginary animal kingdom in Africa that

included **Simba, Mufasa, Nala,** and **Scar**, and the songs *"Circle of Life"* and *Hakuna Matata:* "Animal Kingdom" or "The Lion King?"

453. If Africa is the second largest continent in the world, which one is the largest?

454. How many countries is Asia made up of: 48 or 22?

455. What is considered to be the *smallest* country in the world: Vatican City near Italy, or Monaco in the south of France?

456. What is the *largest* country in the world: Canada or Russia?

457. What is the third largest country after Russia and Canada: The United States or China?

458. What best describes the historical time periods of China: dynasties or regimes?

459. What is the name of the first emperor of China that founded the Qin Dynasty: Qin Shi Huang or Liu Xin?

460. While Emperor of China, was Qin Shi Huang credited with establishing several provinces within the country, a central government, a common currency, a common system of writing, and improving the infrastructure of China with new roads and canals?

461. What large **stone structure** now extending 5,500 miles long and now considered one of the new wonders of the world did Qin Shi Huang begin construction on, with more than one million workers in order to protect China from northern invaders?

462. What is the name of the **baked clay** that was used to build the 8,000 sculptures representing the armies of the first emperor of China, Qin Shi Huang: adobe or terracotta?

463. What is the name of the *dynasty* that followed the harsh rule of the Qin Dynasty when the peasants revolted and killed Emperor Qin: Ming Dynasty or Han Dynasty?

464. Did Liu Bang change his name to Han Gaozu when he founded and became the Emperor of the Han Dynasty?

465. Is the Han Dynasty credited with the inventions of paper, crop rotation, and iron casting?

466. What is the name for the *social code of behavior* and the philosopher whose ideas were followed during the Han Dynasty: Copernicus or Confucius?

467. What is the name for the administrative system of the Chinese government that began with the Han Dynasty, lasted for over 2,000 years, and created educated government workers who were required to pass a difficult exam: civil service or military service?

468. Did **Confucius** have a philosophy of always treating others with respect, along with other rules for good behavior?

469. What did the **Han Emperors** establish in order that the people would be educated and intelligent: schools or writing tablets?

470. What is the name of the **fabric** originally from China that comes from the cocoons of silkworms, and was an important trade product?

471. Did the Chinese Emperors want to keep the *silk-making* process a secret and were they successful for over 1,000 years?

472. What was the most popular embroidered design on silk clothing: birds and flowers, or animals and stripes?

473. What was a symbol of status in China: clothing or jewelry?

474. Would a person wearing silk more likely be from the upper class or the lower class?

475. What was the name of the **trade route** between China and the East and the Mediterranean that was a great source of wealth for them: the Silk Road or the Textile Trail?

476. Was the **Silk Road** important for trade and commerce, or for traveling to other parts of Asia?

477. Were many silk paintings and sculptures created during the Han Dynasty?

478. What was the name of the religion that many Chinese people followed during the Han Dynasty that focused on a new awakening: Buddhism or Taoism?

479. What Chinese dynasty followed the Han and then the Sui Dynasty: Tang or Ming?

480. What industry was important during the Tang Dynasty, transporting silk, pearls, spices, and fine porcelains from one place to another in caravans: trading or road-building?

481. What animal would the Chinese travel on in a **caravan** on the trade route: a horse or a camel?

482. What was invented during the Tang Dynasty that allowed for the mass production of a book: woodblock printing or the printing press?

483. What is the first full-length thing that was produced using Chinese woodblock printing?

484. What product was invented in its early form during the Tang Dynasty that they would use for fireworks because they believed that it scared off evil spirits: dynamite or gunpowder?

485. What is the name of the Chinese **ceramic** that was developed during the Tang Dynasty: Porcelain or Bone China?

486. What **genre** of literature besides the writing of short stories became very widespread and was a very important aspect of Chinese culture during the Tang Dynasty: novels or poetry?

487. What religion was followed after Buddhism lost its place during the Tang Dynasty: Confucianism or Islam?

488. What **hot drink** became popular during the Tang Dynasty: coffee or tea?

489. What type of **paper** that is used in the bathroom was invented during the Tang Dynasty?

490. What kind of **money** was first developed and used during the Tang Dynasty: coins or paper?

491. What great structure in China continued to be built and re-built to keep out northern invaders during the Tang Dynasty?

492. Did the *Song Dynasty* come before or after the Tang Dynasty?

493. What two things were invented during the *Song Dynasty*: the magnetic compass and the iron plow, or the clock and the wheel?

494. What was printed in great quantities through a newly invented process called *moveable type* that made it possible for more people in China to read?

495. Was the *Song Dynasty* one of the most advanced civilizations in the world?

496. What product became an import **crop** during the Song Dynasty, yielding two harvests per year: corn or rice?

497. What type of **architecture** was popular during the Song Dynasty: imperial palaces or tall pagodas?

498. What is the name of the country to the north of China: India or Mongolia?

499. What is the name of the desert located in Mongolia: Mojave or Gobi?

500. Which civilization invented writing, the magnetic compass, gunpowder, the boat rudder, moveable sails, the mechanical clock, the umbrella, porcelain, the wheelbarrow, the spinning wheel, moveable type, seismographs, stirrups, matches, acupuncture, paper money, kites, tea, and ice cream: the Mongolians or the Chinese?

501. What is the name of the **calculator** that was invented by the Chinese that used sliding beads to compute equations: the abacus or the compass?

502. When Khan from Mongolia defeated the Chinese Emperor and became the new Emperor of China, what city did he establish as his home, and this city is still the capital of China today: Hong Kong or Beijing?

503. What did the ***Mongol Emperors*** establish to promote caravan trade over long distances whereby sellers of silks, spices, porcelains and other products could travel in a single caravan with minimal risk of losing profits: merchant associations or trade associations?

504. What is the name of the ***Italian explorer*** and trader who traveled over 24 years throughout China trading jewels and lamp oil: Marco Polo or Lawrence of Arabia?

505. What road did Marco Polo travel along in China: The Silk Road or the Imperial Parkway?

506. What is the name of the dynasty after the Mongols were driven out of China, was led by a self-appointed emperor named Zhu, and lasted three centuries: Ming or Zheng?

507. What specific **handiwork** is the Ming Dynasty known for: porcelain pottery or woodcarvings?'

508. What **color** is Ming porcelain pottery before it is glazed: brown or white?

509. What color was the preferred colored glaze to paint on the porcelain vases: blue or red?

510. What did Europeans call the Ming porcelain that they traded for: pottery or china?

511. What **fabric** did Chinese artists paint birds, animals, and landscapes on: canvas or silk scrolls?

512. What is the name of the art of *fancy handwriting* of the Chinese that uses brushes and ink to make pictures and symbols: cursive or calligraphy?

513. What did the Chinese consider calligraphy, poetry, and painting: the Three Perfections or the Three Arts?

514. What did the Chinese often use in their artworks: lacquer or oil paint?

515. What is regarded as the highest form of Chinese painting: birds or landscapes?

516. What is the name of the 5,500 mile-long **wall** with over 7,000 lockout towers that the Ming Dynasty peasants helped to complete with bricks?

517. Is the Great Wall of China regarded as the *longest* or the *widest* man-made structure in the world?

518. What hauling machine did the Chinese invent to help them build the Great Wall of China: the wheelbarrow or the shovel?

519. What is the name of the Chinese **canal** built during the Ming Dynasty that helped the trade industry in China, and is the world's longest artificial river: Great Canal or Grand Canal?

520. What is another name for the *imperial palace* built by emperors in Beijing China, considered the largest ancient palace in the world: the Taj Mahal or the Forbidden City?

521. What Chinese building also served as a **fortress** complete with a moat, lookout towers, and guards: Imperial Palace or Chinese Temple?

522. How many Chinese Emperors lived in the Imperial Palace over 500 years: 5 or 24?

523. Did China have a fleet of explorer ships under the Chinese Admiral Zheng He before or after Columbus and his voyages in 1492?

524. Which countries did Zheng He help to establish trade with as the commander of his treasure ship voyages: India and Africa, or America and Canada?

525. What were Taoism, Confucianism, and Buddhism: religions or philosophies?

526. What is the name of the country south of China, the birthplace of Buddha in 563 BC, whose teachings emphasize the rebirth of the self: Mongolia or Nepal?

527. What is the name for the *Taoism* philosophy that everything in nature has two balancing forces like hot and cold or dark and light: Yin and Yang or Feng Shui?

528. What is the name for the Chinese system for positioning a structure or the objects within a structure in such a way as to be in harmony with spiritual forces: Yin and Yang or Feng Shui?

529. What are the two major rivers in China: the Yellow and the Yangtze, or the Tigres and Euphrates?

530. What animal is the symbol of power and good luck in China: the panda or the dragon?

531. Who is the *dragon* a symbol of: imperial power or the Chinese New Year?

532. Which holiday is the biggest holiday for the Chinese: Christmas or the New Year?

533. What utensil does the Chinese use to eat with: silverware or chopsticks?

534. What is the name of a tall grass with a hollow stem that the Chinese use to make furniture, buildings, and musical instruments: bamboo or sugar cane?

535. What animal lives near the Yangtze River in China, eats bamboo, and is considered an endangered species: the Giant Panda or the Siberian Tiger?

536. Where are many ginseng plants and bonsai trees grown: Nepal or China?

537. What number is considered lucky in Chinese culture: two or four?

538. What is each year in the Chinese calendar named after: a flower or an animal?

539. What is the name of the major mountain range in China: the Himalayas or the Pyrenees?

540. What is the name of the **tallest** mountain on Earth located between China and Nepal: Mt. McKinley or Mt. Everest?

541. What is considered to be the second tallest mountain on Earth located on the border between China and Pakistan: Mt Everest or K2?

542. What is the most populous country on Earth: Russia or China?

543. What is the official name for China: The People's Republic of China or The Emperor's Republic of China?

544. What is the name for the place on the southern coast of China that is considered a special administrative region, is an important port for exporting goods, and has several attractions including Ocean Park, Victoria Bay, Victoria Peak and Disneyland: Shanghai or Hong Kong?

545. Is China a Communist country where the Chinese government controls all economic activity and the people are given little power to elect officials, or a Republic country where the people have the power to elect government officials?

546. What is the current **capital** of China: Beijing or Shanghai?

547. What is the name of the *square* in the center of Beijing that is named for the gate that is located to the north of the square, separating it from the Forbidden City: Tiananmen Square or Beijing Square?

548. What is the most populated city of China: Beijing or Shanghai?

549. What is the name of the official language of China: Cantonese or Mandarin?

550. How many main groups of Chinese dialects are there in China: seven or twelve?

551. Do many Chinese people also speak English?

552. Is the Chinese language written with letters or with symbols?

553. What cuisine would the following foods be categorized as: wonton soup, Peking duck, rice, noodles, egg rolls, dumplings, tofu, tea, and stir-fry prepared in a large pan called a wok?

554. What article of clothing is traditionally removed before entering a house in an Asian country?

555. What are the two main Chinese folk dances called: the Lion Dance and the Dragon Dance, or the Tiger Dance and the Panda Dance?

556. What is the name of the *martial art* that originated in ancient China and is still widely practiced today: Kung Fu or Karate?

557. What is the name for the *twelve Chinese animal signs* that symbolize when a person was born that include a rat, an ox, a tiger, a rabbit, a dragon, a snake, a horse, a sheep, a monkey, a rooster, a dog, and a pig: zodiac or horoscope?

558. In the year 1492, who "sailed the ocean blue?"

559. What is the century of the 1500's called because it was the time of European explorers and conquerors like Hernán Cortés, Ferdinand Magellan, Francisco Pizarro, and Sir Walter Raleigh who founded the first English colony in North America: the Reformation or the Age of Discovery?

560. Which period is known as the time of writers like *Miguel Cervantes* and *William Shakespeare,* scientists like *Johannes Kepler, Galileo Galilei,* and *Isaac Newton*, conflicts in England regarding the monarchy and religion, the establishment of Jamestown, and the arrival of the Pilgrims on the Mayflower from England to Plymouth, Massachusetts: 1600's or 1700's?

561. Which country ruled the American colonies in the 1700's: France or Great Britain?

562. What is the name of the war between 1754 and 1763 that arose over a dispute regarding land in the Ohio Valley, when the British defeated the French and the Native American Indians: the French and British War or the French and Indian War?

563. What was the French and Indian War referred to as in England: the French and Indian War, or the Seven Years War?

564. What did Britain want to collect from the American colonists in order to help pay for the costs of the French and Indian War: land treaties or taxes?

565. What became the rally cry of the colonists who felt that the British government did not have the right to tax them given that the colonists did not have any of their own representatives in the British Parliament: "taxation without representation" or "unfair tax act?"

566. What was the name of the tax law that the British government passed in 1765 that required the colonists to pay a tax on all printed materials like newspapers and legal documents, and had an official British seal on it that was proof that the tax was paid: the Tax Act or the Stamp Act?

567. Did the colonies willingly pay the taxes to the British, or did they protest and boycott British products?

568. What was the name of the *congress* formed by the American colonies that gathered in 1765 with the goal of preparing a formal protest of the British taxes: The Stamp Act Congress or the Colonial Congress?

569. What was the name of the groups formed by some American patriots led by Samuel Adams that opposed the taxes on them by the British Parliament, and wanted to protect the rights of the colonists: The Colonies for Fair Representation, or the Sons of Liberty?

570. What was the name of the new series of tax laws, established in 1767 by Britain on American colonists that placed a tax on paper, tea, glass, and paint: The Colonial Tax Act or the Townshend Acts?

571. Did the colonists *accept* the taxes as established by the Townshend Acts, or did the colonists protest and start to rebel because they felt that these tax laws violated their rights?

572. What was the name of the event in 1770 that occurred when the tension between 50 colonists and British soldiers that were gathered outside the Custom House in Boston became so high that the soldiers fired into the crowd killing five colonists: the Boston Tea Party or the Boston Massacre?

573. What was the name of the *protest* in 1773 by the American colonists against Britain's new law that only the high priced tea of the British East India Company could be sold in America, and so they proceeded to dress up like Native American Mohawk Indians, board three ships in Boston Harbor, and throw 342 crates of valuable tea into the water: the Boston Tea Protest or the Boston Tea Party?

574. What was the name given by American patriots to the new set of *five laws* that were passed by Britain's Parliament in 1774 as punishment for the Boston Tea Party, included closing Boston Harbor that further limited the rights of the colonists: the Townshend Acts or the Intolerable Acts?

575. What was the name of the first assembly of 12 representatives from the colonies that met in Philadelphia in 1774 to write a letter to King George III of England demanding that he repeal the new taxes of the Intolerable Acts, as well as to make a plan to meet again in May of 1775 if their demands were not met: The First Colonial Congress or the First Continental Congress?

576. Which founding father and member of the First Continental Congress made the statement in 1775, *"I am not a Virginian, I am an American,"* and rallied his people to join Massachusetts against the British with his famous speech that ended with, *"give me liberty or give me death:"* John Adams or Patrick Henry?

577. What was the name of the famous *pamphlet* written by Thomas Paine in 1776 that demanded complete independence from Britain, and quickly sold over 100,000 copies in a few months: Patrick Henry or Thomas Paine?

578. Who is credited for saying, *"lead, follow, or get out of the way:"* Thomas Paine or George Washington?

579. What was the term for the people who wanted the American colonies to gain their independence from Britain, and included Thomas Jefferson, John Adams, Benjamin Franklin, George Washington, and Samuel Adams: loyalists or patriots?

580. What are American patriots like Washington, Jefferson, Adams, and Franklin also regarded as: Founding Fathers or Revolutionaries?

581. What was the term for the people who lived in the American colonies who wanted to remain British citizens and remain loyal to the king: patriots or loyalists?

582. What were the two places in Massachusetts that the colonists concealed their guns and ammunition in preparation for the war with the British: Boston and Bunker Hill or Lexington and Concord?

583. Were the *Sons of Liberty* and the colonists keeping an eye on the British in case they needed to warn other colonists of an attack?

584. What was the name of the rider whose job it was to cross the Charles River on horseback to Charleston and then Lexington

to warn John Hancock and Samuel Adams that the British were coming, during his famous *"midnight ride:"* Paul Revere or Patrick Henry?

585. What was the name of the other rider that set out to warn the colonists so that they would be prepared and could better fight off a British attack: Patrick Henry or William Dawes?

586. What did the colonist Robert Newman display in the steeple of the Old North Church on the night of April 18th 1775 as a warning to the colonists how the British would attack, *"one if by land, two if by sea,"* the "sea" being the Charles River: candles or lanterns?

587. What was the common way to refer to the British troops because of the bright red uniforms they wore: Redcoats or Redjackets?

588. What did Revere and Dawes yell as a warning to their fellow patriots: *"the British are coming," "the Redcoats are coming,"* or neither, as they did not want to risk getting caught?

589. What were the two battles that signaled the start of the Revolutionary War: Boston and Bunker Hill, or Lexington and Concord?

590. Did Samuel Adams and John Hancock manage to escape the British in Lexington thanks to the warnings of Paul Revere?

591. What was another name for *American militiamen,* so called because they could be ready to fight with just a moment's notice: Militiamen or Minutemen?

592. Did the American side have both a militia of ordinary citizens and a Continental Army of trained soldiers?

593. What was the main *weapon* during the Revolutionary War: bows or muskets?

594. Where was the first shot fired that later became known as ***"the shot heard around the world,"*** written in a poem by Ralph Waldo Emerson: Concord or Lexington?

595. Who was the first shot fired by in Lexington: a Redcoat, a Minuteman, or is it still uncertain?

596. Which side won battle at the North Bridge in Concord: the British or the Americans?

597. What city were the British forced to retreat to: Lexington or Boston?

598. Who led the British troops: Lieutenant Colonel Francis Smith or Captain John Parker?

599. Who led American troops: Lieutenant Colonel Francis Smith or Captain John Parker?

600. What were the names of the *two hills* that the British wanted to control so that they would have a tactical advantage and maintain control of the seaports: Bunker and Breeds, or Concord and Lexington?

601. Did the Battle of Bunker Hill actually take place on that hill, or did it take place on Breeds Hill, that was called mistakenly called *Bunker Hill* by the British army?

602. Which side ultimately won the *Battle of Bunker Hill* in part because the other side ran out of ammunition, and claimed victory even though it had more casualties and wounded: British or American?

603. What were the American soldiers told by their commanders because they were so low on ammunition: "Do not fire until

you see the whites of their eyes," or, "Do not fire until you see the reds of their coats?"

604. Which side had 30,000 professional soldiers to the other side's 15,000 colonial farmers, and 270 navy ships to the other side's eight: the British or the Americans?

605. What were two *advantages* of the American side: ammunition and weapons, or knowledge of the land and determination for freedom?

606. What is the name of the *congress*, led by John Hancock that met in order to discuss further strategy to form an army, fight the British, and declare their independence: the Second American Congress, or the Second Continental Congress?

607. Who did the members of the Second Continental Congress elect in 1775 as the General of the Continental Army: George Washington or Benjamin Franklin?

608. What bird did John Adams and Thomas Jefferson, members of the Continental Congress, chose to symbolize the United States: the hawk or the eagle?

609. How many African Americans fought in the Continental Army: 500 or 5,000?

610. Which representative was chosen by the *Second Continental Congress* and the members of the Committee of Five to write the first draft of the letter that would declare the United States independent from Britain: Benjamin Franklin or Thomas Jefferson?

611. What is the date that the final version of the **Declaration of Independence** was adopted by the Second Continental Congress: July 4, 1776 or June 11, 1776?

612. On what date does American celebrate its independence every year?

613. How many members of the Congress signed the Declaration of Independence: 38 or 56?

614. Who was the first congress member to write his *signature,* five inches long, on the Declaration of Independence: George Washington or John Hancock?

615. Were copies of the Declaration of Independence sent to all thirteen colonies as well as to Britain?

616. Does the Declaration essentially declare that all states in North America be free and independent states, and that America was its own free country moving forward?

617. Where is the *original* Declaration of Independence on display today: the Smithsonian Institution or the National Archives?

618. Was the Revolutionary war still going on *after* the signing of the Declaration?

619. What did George Washington offer to encourage more people to join the troops: money, land, or money **and** land?

620. What is the name of the **river** that George Washington crossed with his army on a snowy, Christmas night in a surprise attack on the British, was a victory for the American troops, and helped to revitalize the Continental Army: Potomac or Delaware?

621. What did the Second Continental Congress decide that the country needed to represent the united colonies that would have thirteen red and white stripes and a blue area with thirteen stars, and passed a Resolution to accomplish this on June 14, 1777?

622. When do we celebrate **Flag Day**, originally observed in Waubeka, Wisconsin at Stoney Hill School in 1885, officially approved as a day national observance by congress, and

signed into law by President John Truman: June 14th or July 4th?

623. Has the American flag gone through many transformations since the original version of 1777?

624. How many stars are on the American flag currently?

625. What are "Old Glory," "The Star-Spangled Banner," and "Stars and Stripes" nicknames for?

626. What is the name of the battle that was won by the American troops in New York in 1777 after the surrender of the British General and over 6,000 British soldiers, and was a turning point in the Revolutionary War for the American side: Yorktown or Saratoga?

627. Which European country did Ben Franklin convince to support the American effort after the Battle of Saratoga, resulting in this country sending military aid to America: France or Spain?

628. What country sent several ships to America in 1778 providing them with weapons and setting up blockades so that the British could not receive supplies?

629. Did many women help out the Revolutionary War effort?

630. What is the name of the war General that helped the Americans win several battles including Saratoga, but was and is regarded as a *traitor* after he changed sides, acted as a spy, and sold American military secrets to the British: Benedict Arnold or Samuel Adams?

631. What is the name of the place near Philadelphia where the Continental Army made their camp during the harsh winter of 1777-1778, and the place where the military leaders of George Washington of the American Continental Army, General von Steuben of Prussia, and General Marquis de

Lafayette of France all helped to train the army: Yorktown or Valley Forge?

632. What is the name of the *last* battle of the American Revolutionary War that took place in Virginia, lasted 20 days, and ended when British General Cornwallis and the out-numbered British army surrendered to Washington and the American troops with the showing of a white flag: Valley Forge or Yorktown?

633. What is the name of the official *peace treaty* between Britain and the United States that was signed on September 3rd, 1783 in France that officially ended the American Revolutionary War, and was finally ratified by King George III of England in 1784: The Treaty of Trent or The Treaty of Paris?

634. What was the name of the war in America between the British and the American Colonists that lasted from 1775-1783?

635. Did each of the thirteen states in the United States have to create and adopt their own state constitution after the Revolutionary War?

636. What document did the members develop that help to establish a central government that was finally ratified by the thirteen states in 1781 and is regarded as our first constitution: The Articles of Confederation or The Bill of Rights?

637. What is the name for the *uprising* that took place in Massachusetts in 1786 by farmers protesting high taxes, tax collectors, and foreclosures on farms that further emphasized the need for a strong central government: Farmers' Revolt or Shays' Rebellion?

638. What is the name of the first *plan* that James Madison of Virginia and other delegates drafted in 1787 in Philadelphia proposing a strong central government while maintaining citizens' basic rights, and contained specific ideas that would become part of the U.S. Constitution: the Virginia Plan, or the Constitution?

639. What is the name for the series of 85 newspaper articles written by James Madison, Alexander Hamilton, and John Jay in 1787 that were published anonymously promoting the ratification of the U.S. Constitution: The Constitution Papers or The Federalist Papers?

640. What is the name of the first ten amendments to the Constitution written by George Mason and James Madison, reflect the American ideals of liberty, a limited government, and the rule of law: The Preamble or The Bill of Rights?

641. What is the name of the ***meeting*** of the delegates of colonial America in 1787 to discuss Madison's Virginia Plan and the structure of the central government, and outlined the roles of the executive branch, the legislative branch, and the judicial branch: The Constitutional Convention or The Philadelphia Convention?

642. Which *branch* of government carries out the laws of the country, and is led by the president: legislative, executive, or judicial?

643. Which *branch* of government includes the justices and the courts, and interprets the laws and the constitution: executive, legislative, or judicial?

644. Which *branch* of government makes the laws, and includes the Senate and the House of Representatives collectively called the Congress: legislative, executive, or judicial?

645. What is the name of the solution to the issue of fair representation in the legislative branch of the government that would give each state equal representation in the Senate and representation in the House of Representatives based on its population: the Connecticut Compromise or the Virginia Compromise?

646. What two bodies make up the United States Congress?

647. How many **senators** does each state have in the Senate: two or four?

648. How many *total* senators are in the United States Senate?

649. How many **House Representatives** does each state have: the number proportional to the population of that state, or four representatives?

650. How many *total* representatives are there in the U.S. House of Representatives: 400 or 435?

651. What is the name of the *compromise* that was reached by the delegates in 1787 at the Constitutional Convention regarding representation based on state population and whether or not that would include slaves, and agreeing that *"free persons"* would count as one, and slaves or *"non-free persons"* would count as three-fifths of a person: The Slavery Compromise or The Three-Fifths Compromise?

652. How many years was proposed by the delegates to wait before passing any new laws that would regulate the slave trade: 10 or 20?

653. What is considered the *supreme* law of the United States and the binding agreement among all people: The Bill of Rights or The U.S. Constitution?

654. What is the name for the introduction to the U.S. Constitution that states: "We the People of the United States,

in order to form a more perfect Union, establish justice, insure domestic tranquility, provide for the common defense, promote the general welfare, and secure the blessings of liberty to ourselves and our posterity, do ordain and establish this Constitution for the United States of America:" The Bill of Rights or The Preamble?

655. What is the name for the system that the writers of the Constitution devised so that each of the three branches of the government *limits* the power of the others, ensuring that no one branch becomes too powerful: checks and balances, or branch monitoring?

656. Does the president have the power to oppose or **"veto"** a law that is passed?

657. In what year was the U.S. Constitution approved by all states: 1776 or 1790?

658. What is the word for a change or an alteration: an amendment or a bill?

659. What is the name for the *first 10 amendments* to the U.S. Constitution: The Preamble or The Bill of Rights?

660. Which amendment in the **Bill of Rights** guarantees the freedom of religion, freedom of speech, freedom of the press, the freedom to assemble, and the freedom to petition: the First Amendment or the Second Amendment?

661. Does each state have a government with the three different branches and a constitution?

662. Who is the executive leader of the United States government: the President or the Congress?

663. Who is leader of the state government: the senator or the governor?

664. What is the name of the current *governor* of the state you live in?

665. Who is the leader of the city government: the mayor or the alderman?

666. What is the name of the current *mayor* of the city you live in?

667. What do we pay to the local, state, and federal governments to run them and pay for schools, roads, and the salaries of public workers: duties or taxes?

668. Is it important for American citizens to participate in some way in the government?

669. Which president stated in 1863 that government should be *"of the people, by the people, and for the people:"* President Lincoln or President Johnson?

670. Who became the first president of the United States in 1789 and is considered to be *"the Father of the Country?"*

671. Who was the first **"First Lady"** of the United States, the wife of George Washington: Martha Washington or Abigail Washington?

672. Who was the first **vice**-president of the United States: John Adams or Thomas Jefferson?

673. What is the term for the group of advisors to the President of the United States: Secretaries or Cabinet?

674. Is the Vice-President of the United States a member of the President's Cabinet?

675. What is the term for each cabinet member in the United States each of whom is in charge of a specific area of government: Secretary or Ambassador?

676. How many executive departments make up the President's cabinet: 10 or 15?

677. What is the name for the Secretary that handles *international* relations: Secretary of State or Secretary of Defense?

678. Are there executive departments led by Secretaries for Agriculture, Education, Defense, Energy, Health, Homeland Security, Labor, State, Transportation, and the Treasury?

679. Is the Attorney General considered part of the President's Cabinet?

680. Who was the Secretary of State to George Washington: Thomas Jefferson or Alexander Hamilton?

681. Who was the Secretary of the Treasury to George Washington: Thomas Jefferson or Alexander Hamilton?

682. How many years are considered one term for a U.S. President: two or four?

683. How many terms is a U.S. President limited to, according to the Constitution: two or four?

684. Do candidates that run for a government typically represent a specific political party?

685. What was the political party of Thomas Jefferson and his followers: Democratic-Republican or Federalist?

686. What was the political party of Alexander Hamilton and his followers: Republican or Federalist?

687. What were the country's first two political parties: Democratic-Republican and Libertarian, or Democratic-Republican and Federalist?

688. What are the two main political parties in the United States currently: Republican and Democrat, or Federalist and Libertarian?

689. What was the first capital of the United States: Boston or New York City?

690. What is the present-day capital of the United States of America?

691. What is the name of the official *residence* of the President of the United States located in Washington D.C. starting with President John Adams?

692. What is the name of Washington's home in Virginia that he retired to after his presidency: Mount Vernon or Monticello?

693. What is the name of the office building in Washington D.C. that houses the United States Congress: the U.S. Capitol or the White House?

694. Who was the second President of the United States: Thomas Jefferson or John Adams?

695. Who was the **Vice**-President to second President John Adams: Madison or Jefferson?

696. What is the name of the wife of John Adams and the mother of our 6th President John Quincy Adams, who believed in equal rights for all people, including women and blacks: Martha Adams or Abigail Adams?

697. Who was the third President of the United States and the principle *author* of the Declaration of Independence: Thomas Jefferson or Alexander Hamilton?

698. Who owned the land west of the Mississippi from Canada to Mexico during the early years of Jefferson's Presidency: France or Spain?

699. What was the name of the French territory named for the King of France, Louis the Fourteenth: St. Louis or Louisiana?

700. Whom did Jefferson ask Secretary James Monroe to talk with in France about the sale of the French territory collectively known as Louisiana: Napoleon Bonaparte or King Louis XIV?

701. What is the name of the *land deal* of 1803 when President Jefferson bought Iowa, Missouri, Arkansas, Nebraska, Kansas, Oklahoma, South Dakota and parts of other states for $15 million dollars from France, nearly doubling the size of the United States: The American Acquisition or The Louisiana Purchase?

702. What two explorers did President Jefferson ask in 1804 to explore the west, the newly purchased Louisiana Territory, and along the way met several Native American Tribes including a Shoshone Indian, Sacajawea, who helped them as an interpreter: Lewis and Clark, or Henry Hudson and Marco Polo?

703. How many years was the expedition of *Lewis and Clark,* and included navigating the Great Falls in Montana as well as the rugged Rocky Mountains while on foot, on horseback, and in canoes: one year or two years?

704. How did Lewis and Clark *document* their findings on their expedition regarding geographical features, the Missouri River, weather, over 180 plant species, and over 120 mammals, reptiles, birds, and fish including grizzly bear, buffalo, woodpeckers, sheep, deer, prairie dogs and trout: kept detailed written journals, or communicated their observations with the Indians?

705. Who was the fourth President of the United States: James Monroe or James Madison?

706. What is the name of the two-year war in the early 1800's between the United States and Britain that arose over trade, shipping and naval law disagreements: The Seven Years War or the War of 1812?

707. What is the name of U.S. naval ship nicknamed *"Old Ironsides,"* that managed to capture 24 enemy ships during the War of 1812: USS Constitution or USS Enterprise?

708. What symbolic building was burned in the Battle of Washington that was re-built and painted white to duplicate the lime-based whitewash that was applied to this building in 1798: The Capitol or The White House?

709. What is the name of the treaty that was signed in 1814 to end the War of 1812 giving the United States a victory: The Treaty of Paris or the Treaty of Ghent?

710. What is the name for the *final* battle of 1812 won convincingly by the Americans, led by General Andrew Jackson, occurring 15 days after the Treaty of Ghent was signed because neither side was aware of the existing peace treaty: The Battle of New Orleans, or The Battle of Louisiana?

711. Who was the **fifth** President of the United States elected in 1816, re-elected in 1820, with a foreign policy doctrine named for him that opposed further European colonization and interference with nations in the western hemisphere: James Monroe or James Madison?

712. Was *slavery* an issue in the colonial America in 1820?

713. Which part of the country owned slaves and depended on them to work on their large plantations and farms: The North or The South?

714. Which part of the country did not own slaves and earned a living by working in factories or managing a small farm: The North or The South?

715. What is the term used to refer to people that wanted to abolish or do away with slavery: revolutionists or abolitionists?

716. What is the name of the *compromise* that served to maintain the balance of slavery between the anti-slavery North and the pro-slavery South that allowed Missouri to enter the Union as a slave state, and Maine to enter the Union as a free state: The Missouri Compromise or The Maine Compromise?

717. What is the name of the *proclamation* by President James Monroe in his address to Congress in 1823 that stated that the United States would not tolerate any European presence, intervention, or colonization in the Western Hemisphere, and that the United States would assume a neutral role in European affairs: The Monroe Plan or The Monroe Doctrine?

718. Who was the sixth President of the United States who opposed slavery, supported freedom of speech, and only served one term: Andrew Jackson or John Quincy Adams?

719. Who was the seventh President of the United States elected in 1828, was a commander in the war of 1812, was known as the *"people's president,"* removed Native American Cherokees from their land, is pictured on the U.S. twenty dollar bill, and the capital of Mississippi is named for him: Andrew Jackson or Andrew Johnson?

720. What was President's Jackson goal regarding Indian land: transfer Indian land into U.S. territory, or allow all Native American Indians to keep their land?

721. What was the name of the *bill* that President Jackson convinced Congress to pass in 1830 that would allow the government to force the Native Americans to Indian Territory more than 1,000 miles away: The Indian Removal Act or The Indian Reservation Act?

722. What was the name given for the *forced relocation* of Native American Cherokee Indians from their homeland of Georgia to the Indian Territory of Oklahoma, and was so named because of the brutal journey that it was: The March of Pain or The Trail of Tears?

723. What is the term for a person that takes action to improve social or economic conditions: reformer or revolutionary?

724. What is the name of the lady that believed in the rights of the mentally ill and their treatment in institutions in the early 1800's: Dorothea Dix or Clara Barton?

725. What is the name of the reformer of American education and worked to improve public schools and the number of children attending those schools: Horace Mann or Dorothea Dix?

726. Who are the two women who believed in equality and women's rights, and organized a convention in Seneca Falls, New York in 1848: Lucretia Mott and Elizabeth Stanton, or Elizabeth Stanton and Amelia Bloomer?

727. What is the name of the editor of a magazine who attended a convention Seneca, New York promoting the right of women to wear comfortable clothing, and had bloomers or the short pants worn under a skirt named for her: Amelia Bloom or Amelia Bloomer?

728. Who is the African American woman abolitionist and women's rights activist who was born into slavery, gained her freedom in 1827, and developed a great following after her 1851 speech, *"Ain't I a Woman,"* at the Ohio Women's Rights Convention: Sojourner Truth or Harriet Tubman?

CHAPTER 3

Civics - 4th Grade

1.   What is the term for the set of rules and regulations set up by the government of a town, city, state, and nation: statutes or laws?

2.   Does America have local, state, and federal laws?

3.   What are the three levels of government: executive, legislative, and judicial, or President, House of Representatives, and Senate?

4.   What is the term for the *national* level of government: federal or local?

5.   Which level of government is in charge of the military, the coining of money, highways, passports, Social Security, income tax, and interstate commerce: state or federal?

6.   Which level of government is in charge of schools, automobile registration, sales tax, and welfare: state or federal?

7.   Which level of government is in charge of police and fire, zoning, roads, trash collection, voter registration, school districts, and property taxes: local or state?

8.   What is the name of the document that declared the United States free from English rule?

9.   Who were James Madison, Alexander Hamilton, Ben Franklin, and George Washington: Founding Fathers or famous inventors?

10.   What is the name of the introduction to the U.S. Constitution that states: "We the People of the United States, in Order to

form a more perfect Union, establish Justice, insure domestic Tranquility, provide for the common defense, promote the general Welfare, and secure the Blessings of Liberty to ourselves and our Prosperity, do ordain and establish this Constitution of the United States of America?"

11. What is the name of a **city law** or rule: an ordinance or a treaty?

12. What is the *supreme law of the land*: The United States Constitution or The Bill of Rights?

13. What is a change to the U.S. Constitution called: an addendum or an amendment?

14. What is the term for the *first ten amendments* to the U.S. Constitution: The Bill of Rights or The Preamble?

15. Which branch of government is made up of the Congress and *makes* the laws: the executive branch or the legislative branch?

16. What are the names of the two chambers that make up the U.S. Congress: The House of Representatives and The Senate, or the legislative branch and the judicial branch?

17. Where does the Congress conduct their sessions in Washington D.C: at the U.S. Capitol, or at the White House?

18. What is the capital of the state you live in?

19. What is the name of the person elected to make laws: a candidate or a legislator?

20. Which branch of government includes the President and the cabinet, and carries out and enforces the laws: the judicial branch or the executive branch?

21. Which branch of government is made up of Supreme Court Justices that interpret the law and the U.S. Constitution: the judicial branch or the legislative branch?

22. What is the name of the policy that ensures that one branch does not have more power than another: Separation of Powers, or Checks and Balances?

23. What is the name of the policy that assigns specific duties to each branch of government, Separation of Powers, or Checks and Balances?

24. Who is the leader of the executive branch: The President or the Speaker of the House?

25. What is the name of the current President of the United States?

26. What is the name of the Vice-President of the United States?

27. What is the name of the President's residence in Washington D.C?

28. Who is the commander-in-chief, the person in charge of the Armed Forces: the President or the Vice-President?

29. What is the name of the avenue where the White House is located in Washington D.C.: Pennsylvania Avenue or Philadelphia Avenue?

30. What is the name of the power a President has to reject or deny a government bill: veto power or executive power?

31. What is the name of the highest court in the United States: Head or Supreme?

32. What is the name of the person who makes an official ruling in a court: a judge or a jury?

33.   What is the name of a group of people who listen to a case in a courtroom and decide whether or not a person is guilty of breaking the law: a committee or a jury?

34.   What two groups make up America's legislative branch called the Congress?

35.   How many members are there in the House of Representatives: 435 or 100?

36.   Does the number of officials elected to Congress depend on the population of each state?

37.   How many elected members are there in the U.S. Senate: 435 or 100?

38.   Does the number of officials elected to the Senate depend on the population of each state, or is it currently set at two per state?

39.   What is the name of the leader of the House of Representatives?

40.   How long is the term of a legislator, a member of Congress: two years or six years?

41.   How many U.S. Senators does each state have?

42.   How long is the term of a United States Senator: two years or six years?

43.   What is the name of a suggested law before it becomes a law: a bill or a proposal?

44.   What is the name of a bill that has been passed by a legislature and signed by an executive?

45.   What is the term for the power given to the executive branch to oppose or reject a bill?

46.   What is the name of the elected person in charge of a city?

47. Do you know the name of the mayor of our city?

48. What is the name of the elected person in charge of a state: a governor or a senator?

49. Do you know the name of the governor of our state?

50. Which level of government include mayors, county executives, and aldermen: local or state?

CHAPTER 4

Science – 4th Grade

1. Does the study of science include physical, life, environmental, Earth, and space sciences?

2. What type of science includes magnetism, electricity, sound, matter, and energy: physical or environmental?

3. Is the mass of an object equal to or greater than the amount of matter the object has?

4. Can matter include both living and nonliving things?

5. What are three most common states of matter?

6. What fourth element is also regarded as a state matter besides solids, liquids, and gases: plasmas or fungi?

7. Are the stars with their gases considered a type of plasma?

8. Are fluorescent lights and neon signs types of man-made plasma of natural plasma?

9. What type of matter is a **rock** that has size and shape and can be broken apart?

10. What type of matter is **water** that can move freely and has no shape of its own?

11. What type of matter is **air** that has no shape of its own and is invisible?

12. What is the name of the **gas** that is lighter than the air and is often used in balloons and parade floats: hydrogen or helium?

13. Can matter change into a different state of matter?

14. How is matter changed when ice is boiled and melts: solid to gas, or solid to liquid?

15. How is matter changed when the *steam* from boiling water turns into water vapor?

16. What is another term for the *water vapor* that escapes from the pot of boiling water: condensation or evaporation?

17. What kind of *engines* were the first locomotives powered by: steam or electricity?

18. What is the term given to water that turns into a gas: evaporation or condensation?

19. What is the term for what may occur when warm air hits the cool surface of the window causing it to look foggy: evaporation or condensation?

20. If the weather is extremely cold, what may form from the condensation on the inside of a window?

21. What chemical change or reddish-brown substance results on a nail or an old bike when iron reacts with the oxygen in the air?

22. Are mass, volume, and density visible or invisible properties of matter?

23. Are magnetism and the ability to float visible or invisible properties of matter?

24. What is the name of an object that would *float* on the water because it is buoyant?

25. What is the name of an object that would *sink* in the water because it weighs more than the amount of water it is displacing?

26. Is all matter made up of small particles called atoms and molecules that are too small to see with the naked eye?

27. How many known elements are there of matter: 58, 118, or 218?

28. What is the name for the *smallest* component of an element, is smaller than a grain of sand, and contains protons, neutrons, and electrons: an atom or a molecule?

29. What do atoms become after they join together: molecules o protons?

30. What is the chemical term given to matter that is made up of only one kind of atom: an element or a substance?

31. Are elements the building blocks of all matter?

32. What is the name of the table that lists all the elements according to the structure of their atoms: Atomic Table or Periodic Table?

33. What is the term for matter that is made up of two or more kinds of atoms linked together: a proton or a compound?

34. What is the fourth element that make up matter according to the Greek thinker *Aristotle:* Earth, air, fire, and _?

35. Is the following statement true or false: All substances that exist in the world are made of chemicals?

36. What is a characteristic of matter called that can be *measured*: a property or a mixture?

37. Can characteristics of matter have either physical or chemical properties?

38. Would solidity, appearance, texture, hardness, density, buoyancy, conductivity, and magnetism be considered chemical or physical properties of a substance?

39. Which properties do you think are easier to recognize: chemical or physical?

40. What is the name of the table that is a chart of all chemical elements that are arranged according to their characteristics?

41. What can all *basic substances* be divided into: metals, semimetals, and _?

42. Can you name something that is made of the metal **copper**?

43. Can you name something that is made of the metal **brass**?

44. Can you name something that is made of the metal **stainless steel**?

45. Can you name something that is made of the metal **bronze**?

46. Can you name something that is made of the metal **nickel**?

47. Can you name something that is made of the metal **gold**?

48. Can you name something that is made of the metal **silver**?

49. Can you name something that is made of the metal **iron**?

50. Can you name something that is made of the **tin**?

51. Can you name something that is made of the metal **aluminum**?

52. If you have a 2-liter bottle of Coke, is the 2 liter a measurement of mass or volume?

53. What is the term for that *amount* that something can hold: volume or capacity?

54. What metric unit is **mass** measured in: grams or liters?

55. What metric unit is **volume** measured in: grams or liters?

56. What *instrument* would you use to measure mass: a scale or a balance?

57. What is the term for the ability to do work: force or energy?

58. What are the two **states** of energy: potential and kinetic, or chemical and thermal?

59. What is the term for **stored up** energy: potential or kinetic?

60. What is the term for the energy a body has, once it is set in motion: potential or kinetic?

61. Can energy be transferred from potential to kinetic?

62. Are nuclear energy, chemical energy, electrical energy, radiant energy, mechanical energy, and thermal energy **forms** of energy or **fields** of energy?

63. When you tip the first domino, what energy is being transformed from one domino to the next: kinetic to potential, or potential to kinetic?

64. What do wind, water, fire, sound, and light all provide: fuel or energy?

65. Which requires more energy: pushing a wheelbarrow or watching television?

66. What is the name of the energy that comes from the Sun: thermal or solar?

67. What is the name of the energy that can make a kite fly, turn a mill, or power a turbine to make electricity: electrical or mechanical?

68. Can energy be stored?

69. What is the name of the energy that is stored in foods, batteries, and fossil fuels like coal or natural gas: chemical or potential?

70. Which of the fossil fuels is the most widely used for energy: coal, natural gas, or oil?

71. What is the name of the energy caused by the movement of electrons that power lights, electronics, and appliances: chemical or electrical?

72. What point of energy do you reach if you swing *back* on a swing: potential or kinetic?

73. What point of energy do you reach if you are swinging *forward* on a swing: potential or kinetic?

74. What type of energy does an object have the higher it is off the ground, due to the pull of gravity: potential or kinetic?

75. When a ball starts to fall when you let it go from the air, what does its potential energy convert to: kinetic or stored?

76. When you are about to slide down a hill on a sled, what energy do you start out with and what does this energy become as you slide down the snowy hill?

77. What is energy called that is caused by the movement of electrons: chemical or electrical?

78. What is the name of the energy necessary for moving or spinning objects like a wheel gear, or the wind that turns a windmill: mechanical or electrical?

79. What type of energy is a *fire* in the fireplace an example of: heat or thermal?

80. What type of energy is cooked food an example of: chemical or electrical?

81. What type of energy is water flowing over a waterfall an example of: gravitational or electrical?

82. What is the name of the energy that is stored in foods, batteries, and fossil fuels like natural gas or coal: electrical or chemical?

83. Can energy be classified as renewable or non-renewable?

84. What type of energy source is water, wind, solar, and geothermal: renewable or non-renewable?

85. What type of energy source is petroleum, coal, natural gas, and nuclear power: renewable or non-renewable?

86. What is the term given for a *push or a pull* that causes an object to move, change speed, change direction, or stop: force or motion?

87. Can force transfer energy?

88. What is the term for a change in position: force or motion?

89. Will an object stay in place until some force sets it in motion?

90. Will an object continue to move until some force slows or stops it?

91. What describes how fast an object is moving: speed or velocity?

92. What can a magnet create that can move an object: a force or a pull?

93. What is the term for what causes things to fall when they are dropped: motion or gravity?

94. Is gravity a force or a motion?

95. Does the Earth's gravity pull the moon, the moon's gravity pull the Earth, or both?

96. What is it called when two equal pushes or pulls cancel each other out: balanced forces or equal forces?

97.   If two classes are playing *tug-o-war* and the center flag does not move, do we say that the forces are equal, balanced, or at equilibrium?

98.   In what position is a *seesaw* when it is at its center of gravity in equilibrium?

99.   What is caused when two objects are rubbed together: inertia or friction?

100. What effect does *friction* have on an object because of the resistance that results: slows it down or speeds it up?

101. Would brakes against a tire or wheel be considered friction?

102. When friction stops motion, what does it create: heat or tension?

103. What is the term that refers to the way things *resist* a change in movement: force, inertia, or motion?

104. What is the name of the principle that reads: "Objects in motion tend to stay in motion and objects at rest tend to stay at rest unless acted on by another force:" the law of inertia or the first law of motion?

105. What is the name of the scientist that is credited for the **laws of motion** regarding objects in motion and at rest: Sir Isaac Newton or Galileo Galilei?

106. What is said to have inspired Newton to study the effects of motion and gravity: when an apple fell out of a tree and hit him on the head, or when he threw a ball up in the air?

107. Can you finish Newton's third law of motion: "*For every action there is an equal and _ ?*"

108. What is the cause of your body continuing to move forward, even with your seatbelt fastened, after the car you are in suddenly brakes: motion, force, or inertia?

109. Do objects with *more* mass have more or less inertia?

110. What do we call the *six basic tools* that use force to help us to do work: simple machines or basic machines?

111. What term do we use when we are talking about a pulley, a lever, an inclined plane, a wedge, a screw, and an axle: simple machines or complex machines?

112. What *simple machine* would describe an object with a thin, sharp edge like a knife, an axe, or a nail: a wedge, a lever, or an axle?

113. What *simple machine* would describe a simple machine make of a long object that rests and turns on a pivot of fulcrum like a crowbar, the back of a hammer, a hand brake on a bicycle, or a seesaw: a lever or an axle?

114. What *simple machine* has a wheel attached to a thin axle like a doorknob, a wheel, a wagon, a skateboard, or a pencil sharpener: a wheel and axle, a lever, or a screw?

115. What *simple machine* is shaped like a ramp that would include a ladder, a playground slide, an escalator, or a stairway: a wheel and axle, a lever, or an inclined plane?

116. What *simple machine* is made of a rope wrapped around a wheel, is used to raise or lower a window blind, to raise or lower the sails on a sailboat, or to hoist or lower a flag: a lever, a wedge, or a pulley?

117. What *simple machine* is an inclined plane with a winding edge called a thread, found on a jar lid, the bottom of a light bulb, or a corkscrew: a screw, an axle, or a lever?

118. What is the name of a machine that is a combination of two or more machines: combined or compound?

119. What is the name given to machines that are made up of more than two simple machines: compound or complex?

120. What kinds of machines are a bicycle, a wheelbarrow, and a pair of scissors: complex or compound?

121. What two simple machines make the *wheelbarrow* a compound machine: lever, pulley, screw, or wheel and axle?

122. What things can you name that are electric?

123. What is the name of the pathway taken by an electric current: a circuit or a series?

124. What type of electrons cause an electric current: positive or negative?

125. What type of circuit allows the movement of electricity: open or closed?

126. Does electricity move through insulators or conductors?

127. Are metals considered insulators or conductors of electricity?

128. Are plastic, rubber, and wood considered insulators or conductors of electricity?

129. What kind of circuit has only one pathway for the current: series or parallel?

130. What kind of circuit has two or more pathways for the current: series or parallel?

131. What type of circuit allows current to pass through: open or closed?

132. What type of circuit does *not* allow current to pass through: open or closed?

133. What kind of circuit will light a bulb: an open circuit or a closed circuit?

134. What kind of circuit would a string of holiday lights be on, where the whole string will go dark if one bulb burns out: a parallel circuit or a series circuit?

135. What is it called when the circuit has more than one pathway for the flow of electrical current, and will remain lit even if one bulb burns out: a series circuit or a parallel circuit?

136. What type of metal are wires often made of, and is a good conductor of electricity?

137. What type of metals do magnets attract: iron, cobalt, or nickel?

138. What kinds of lines are created when iron filings line up with a magnetic force: electromagnetic lines or polar lines?

139. Do *dry-celled* batteries generally have low or high voltage?

140. What does a magnetic field create: current or voltage?

141. What type of current do most electronics use: Alternating Current **(AC)**, or Direct Current **(DC)**?

142. What type of current is often used for power lines: AC or DC?

143. What is the *standard unit of measurement* for current: amperes or volts?

144. What kind of electricity would you create if you rub a balloon on a wool sweater or rub your feet on a carpet: static or friction?

145. Is static electricity the result of positively or negatively charged electrons that rub off on a surface?

146. What would you create if you wrapped wire around a nail and ran electricity through it: a magnet, a magnetic field, or an electromagnet?

147. Do some *trains* in the world run on guide rails that use electromagnetic energy?

148. What kind of magnets do *cranes* use to move tons of steel from one place to another?

149. What kind of electricity did Ben Franklin state that lightning was: static or electric?

150. Can electrical energy be transformed into *other* energies including heat, light, or mechanical energy?

151. What is the name of the scientist who in 1831 demonstrated electromagnetic induction by passing a magnet through a coil of wire: Benjamin Franklin or Michael Faraday?

152. What is the name of the scientist who in the 1870's built an electric generator and demonstrated electric lighting in America: Benjamin Franklin or Thomas Edison?

153. What is the name of the scientist who in 1752 flew a kite with a metal tip into a thunderstorm to prove that lightning was a form of electricity, and went on to invent the lightning rod and conductor: Benjamin Franklin or Thomas Edison?

154. Who invented the light bulb, the phonograph, the microphone, and the movie camera?

155. What is the scientific term that refers to the *visible* spectrum of electromagnetic radiation, and may include ultraviolet, infrared, color, optics, speed, and the Sun?

156. What type of light can reach a depth of 280 in the ocean: sunlight or ultraviolet light?

157. What kind of light is a *combination* of different wavelengths of light traveling together: visible or invisible?

158. Are the wavelengths of light represented by **ROYGBIV**, the colors of the visible spectrum and the colors in the rainbow?

159. What does **ROY G BIV** stand for?

160. Which color has the *longest* wavelength in a visible spectrum: red or violet?

161. Which color has the *shortest* wavelength in a visible spectrum: red or violet?

162. Can light be reflected, absorbed, and transmitted?

163. Is the color of an object the color it reflects, or the color it absorbs?

164. Does an *apple* appear red because it reflects the color red and absorbs all other colors?

165. How does **light** travel: in waves or in crescents?

166. What is the combination of several wavelengths of light traveling together: black light or white light?

167. What is the term for the *invisible* electromagnetic radiation in the ultraviolet area of the spectrum: black light or white light?

168. Which two of the following describe the parts of a wave: a crest, a valley, or a trough?

169. Is the crest, the top part of a wave, the same thing as a peak?

170. What is the distance from the crest of one wave to the crest of the next wave: a frequency or a wavelength?

171. What is the bottom of a wave called: a crest or a trough?

172. What is the top of a wave called: a crest or a trough?

173. What kind of radio wave would be used to detect the position of objects that are far away: microwaves or radar?

174. How long does it take for the Sun to travel 93 million miles to Earth: 8 minutes or 8 seconds?

175. Which travels faster: light or sound?

176. Why do you see lightning *before* you hear thunder?

177. What medium can light travel through the fastest: a vacuum, a solid, a liquid, or a gas?

178. Which needs a *medium*, like air or water, to travel through: light or sound?

179. Can sound travel through solids, liquids, and gases?

180. Which travels at a rate of 186,282 miles per second: light or sound?

181. What kind of light is used during *eye* surgery: laser or neon?

182. What living things can see *ultraviolet* light: insects or humans?

183. What kind of surface *reflects* light: smooth or rough?

184. Which travels in straight paths called rays: sound or light?

185. When light hits something in its path and bounces off, is that light reflected or refracted?

186. When light is bent, is it reflected or refracted?

187. Can light be absorbed as heat?

188. When light passes through a surface or an object, is it refracted or transmitted?

189. What do the terms transparent, translucent, and opaque refer to: the amount of light that passes through an object, or the amount of light that is absorbed by an object?

190. What type of material, such as glass, can you see through because it allows light to pass through it: transparent or translucent?

191. What type of material, like tissue paper, allows some light to pass through, but scatters the light in different directions making it appear fuzzy: transparent or translucent?

192. What type of material, such as wood, blocks light *completely* so you cannot see through it: translucent or opaque?

193. Is light that has **not** been transmitted or reflected absorbed or refracted?

194. Will a **clear** glass window reflect or absorb light?

195. What kind of clothing *absorbs* light: dark or light?

196. Would *frosted* glass and tissue paper be translucent or transparent?

197. Would *window* glass and air be translucent or transparent?

198. Would a brick wall and a desktop be opaque or translucent?

199. What is the name for the **curved** piece of glass or plastic that serves to refract light: lens or mirror?

200. What do telescopes, glasses, projectors, goggles, cameras, and microscopes all have?

201. What is it called when the light that passes through a medium like air or water bends: reflection or refraction?

202. How are lenses classified when referring to the *curve* of the glass on each side of the lens: convex and concave, or convergent and divergent?

203. How are lenses classified when referring to *how* the lens bends the light: convex and concave, or convergent and divergent?

204. What kind of lens is *thicker* in the middle than at the edges, and focuses the light that passes through it: concave of convex?

205. What kind of lens is *thinner* in the middle than at the edges, and spreads the light that passes through it: concave or convex?

206. What kinds of lenses are used to make small things appear larger: concave or convex?

207. What kinds of lenses are used to make objects seem smaller and farther away: concave or convex?

208. What kind of lens does a magnifying glass have: concave or convex?

209. What is the name of the *optical* instrument that uses convex lenses in order to see cells and microorganisms?

210. What is the name of the scientific instrument that uses convex lenses to magnify stars and constellations?

211. What is the name of the *handheld* instrument composed of two telescopes and a focusing device that is used to magnify objects?

212. What is the name for the form of energy that is produced and transmitted by *vibrating* matter: light or sound?

213. How does sound travel: in waves or in decibels?

214. Can sound be described in terms of wavelength and frequency?

215. Is the number of wavelengths in a given amount of time a measurement of the frequency of sound or the pitch of sound?

216. What is the frequency of sound measured in: decibels or Hertz?

217. What is the distance between two compressions: the wavelength of sound or the frequency of sound?

218. What is the term for the *depth* of a tone or sound: pitch or vibration?

219. What sound waves would create a *higher* pitch: fast or slow?

220. What sound waves would create a *lower* pitch: fast or slow?

221. Would a big, heavy guitar string create a low pitch or a high pitch when plucked?

222. Would a thin, lighter guitar string create a low pitch or a high pitch when plucked?

223. Does sound travel quicker or slower through solids because the molecules of a solid are closer together?

224. What type matter does sound travel the slowest because the molecules are the farthest apart: solids, liquids, or gases?

225. In which medium would sound travel the fastest: air, water, or steel?

226. Do animals make and hear ranges of sound vibrations differently than humans can make and hear?

227. What do musical instruments do to produce sound: vibrate or compress?

228. What is the measure of the *loudness* of sound: pitch or volume?

229. What is the *volume* of sound measured in: decibels or Hertz?

230. What is it called when you yell something in a canyon, and the reflection of your own sound waves comes back to you?

231. What status do airplanes reach when they *"break"* the sound barrier and create a sonic boom: Mach 1 or supersonic?

232. What part of our bodies take in sound waves?

233. What is the name for the *study* of living things and life processes: Life Science or Earth Science?

234. What are all living things made of: cells or elements?

235. How are living things categorized: as classes or as kingdoms?

236. What are the Monera, Protist, Fungi, Plant, and Animal all classified as: domains or kingdoms?

237. What living things are found on land and water, have been on Earth for millions of years, contain chlorophyll, convert energy through photosynthesis, have a cell wall made of cellulose, and are stationary?

238. What is an example of a plant?

239. How can plants be categorized: vascular and nonvascular, or seed plants and spore plants?

240. Do the plant groups include those that produce seeds and those that produce spores?

241. Would ferns and mosses be spore-producing or seed-producing plants?

242. Would plants having roots, stems, flowers, and leaves be spore-producing or seed- producing plants?

243. Do conifers like pine trees, spruces, and junipers reproduce from spores or from seeds?

244. What category do the majority of plants, trees, shrubs, vines, fruits, and vegetables belong to: flowering or non-flowering?

245. What part of the plant is the part right *under* the developing flower: the leaves or the sepals?

246. What is the process called by which green plants use chlorophyll to produce food and oxygen using carbon dioxide, water, nutrients, and sunlight: pollination or photosynthesis?

247. What is the reproductive process of plants called by which pollen is transferred from the stamens to the stigma: pollination or photosynthesis?

248. What process are pollination, the stamen, the pistil, the sepal, the embryo, the spore, and the seed all a part of: plant reproduction or plant photosynthesis?

249. Are plants producers or consumers?

250. Which part of the plant absorbs nutrients and water from the soil: stem or root?

251. Which part of the plant makes food for the plant: the roots or the leaves?

252. Which part of the plant allows for the movement of water and nutrients and is the part that supports the plant?

253. In what female reproductive part of a flower do the seeds form, found inside the ring of petals: the pistil or the stamen?

254. In what part of a male reproductive flower does pollen form: the pistil or the stamen?

255. What is the name of the process when *pollen* is transferred from the stamen to the pistil?

256. What do mosses and ferns reproduce with: spores or sepals?

257. What is the process called whereby green plants produce their own food?

258. What do green plants produce using chlorophyll, carbon dioxide, water, and sunlight?

259. From what source do plants get their energy?

260. What is the name of the substance that gives plants their *green* color: chlorophyll or pigment?

261. What is the term for the plant stage in the winter, similar to some animals, when all their regular activities stop: hibernation or dormancy?

262. What is the *variable* in an experiment to measure how different kinds of soil affect the growth of a tulip if you put a tulip bulb in four identical pots with four different kinds of soil: the pots, the soil, or the bulbs?

263. If the pots, tulip bulbs, sunlight, and water are exactly the same, would these be considered the *variables* or the *constants*?

264. What is the name given to organisms that get their energy by eating other animals and plants: consumers or producers?

265. What is the term used for organisms like plants that can make their own food: producers or consumers?

266. What is the term for organisms that eat away at dead organic matter: consumers or decomposers?

267. Would *fungi* that can break down organisms and recycle them back to the nutrient pool be considered a producer, consumer, or a decomposer?

268. What is the *order* of the energy cycle from the following: decomposer, Sun, consumer, and producer?

269. What is the name of the system in the environment that is made of all living and non-living things: an ecosystem or a kingdom?

270. What is a *synonym* of an ecosystem: a biome or a kingdom?

271. What is one way that an ecosystem can be destroyed by humans?

272. What is the name of the web that is made up of the *interrelated* food system in an ecosystem: food chain or life cycle?

273. What do food chains and food webs always start with: the Sun or the plant?

274. What is the term for an organism's *role* in a community: status or niche?

275. What is the term for the *environmental area* inhabited by a particular species of plant, animal, or another organism: niche or habitat?

276. What is the term that refers to the *change* by which a specific organism becomes better suited to its present surroundings: adjustment or adaptation?

277. Would adaptations that organisms do like migration, hibernation, or instinct be structural or behavioral?

278. Would adaptations that organisms have like webbed feet, long beaks, camouflaged bodies, etc. be structural or behavioral?

279. What is the name of the study of our planet below the surface, on the surface, and in space: Earth Science or Life Science?

280. What is the name of our system of Sun and planets?

281. What do the words *solar*, *solstice*, and *solarium* all have to do with?

282. How many known, official planets are there?

283. What is **Pluto** now categorized as: a dwarf planet or a meteorite?

284. What have astronomers recently discovered at the edge of our solar system: another dwarf planet or another galaxy?

285. Are Earth, Venus, Mercury, and Mars inner or outer planets?

286. Are Jupiter, Saturn, Neptune, and Uranus inner or outer planets?

287. Is the Earth the second, third, or fourth planet from the Sun?

288. How old is the Earth estimated to be: 2.6 billion, 3.6 billion, or 4.5 billion years old?

289. How many million kilometers away is the Earth from the Sun: 100, 150, or 200?

290. How many million miles away is the Earth from the Sun on average: 73, 83, or 93?

291. What is the name of the layer in Earth's atmosphere that helps protect it from the Sun's ultraviolet rays: the ozone layer or the stratosphere?

292. What three things does the Earth have to help it support life: atmosphere, water, and energy, or water, soil, and oxygen?

293. What did the Ancient Greeks like *Ptolemy* and *Aristotle* believe was the center of our solar system, around which the sun and the planets revolve: the Earth or the Sun?

294. What did the scientists *Galileo* and *Copernicus* believe was the **center** of our solar system, around which all planets revolve: the Earth or the Sun?

295. What is the name of the **star** located 93 million miles away that is over 100 times the diameter of the Earth?

296. How many billion years old is the Sun estimated to be: 3.6, 4.6, or 5.6?

297. How many revolutions or orbits does the Earth make around the Sun every year?

298. How many hours does it take the Earth to make one rotation on its axis?

299. What is the effect of the Earth's rotation on its axis: the seasons, or day and night?

300. What season is it when the hemisphere tilted *toward* the Sun receives the rays more directly, and has longer days and warmer temperatures?

301. What season is it when the hemisphere tilted *away* from the Sun receives the rays less directly, and has shorter days and cooler temperatures?

302. If it is winter in the northern hemisphere, what season is it in the southern hemisphere?

303. To what celestial body did the National Aeronautics Space Agency, known as **NASA**, send astronauts to on its Apollo missions?

304. To which planet did NASA send a camera navigation rover called *"Curiosity"* to look for signs of life?"

305. What is the name of the rocky *satellite* that is about one-quarter the size of the Earth that has no water, no atmosphere, and no known life?

306. What do new, waxing crescent, first quarter, waxing gibbous, full, waning gibbous, last quarter, and waning crescent all refer to: moon phases or moon stages?

307. What is caused and controlled by the Sun and moon's gravitation pull, affecting the rise and fall of an ocean's water levels: tides or eclipses?

308. What type of eclipse occurs when the moon moves *into* the Earth's shadow: solar or lunar?

309. What type of eclipse occurs when the moon passes *between* the Earth and the Sun: solar or lunar?

310. How many layers does the Earth have: three or four?

311. Which of the following is not one of the Earth's layers: crust, mantle, lithosphere, outer core, or inner core?

312. What is the *inner* most layer of the Earth called, estimated to be the size of the moon and hotter than the surface of the Sun: the crust or the inner core?

313. What is the *outer* most layer of the Earth called that is about 25 miles deep: the crust or the mantle?

314. What is the *second* layer of the Earth called which is 1,800 miles of hot magma or molten rock: the outer core or the mantle?

315. What is the *third* layer of the Earth called which is made of hot liquid metal: the inner core or the outer core?

316. What is the name for the *innermost* layer Earth, measuring nearly 4,000 feet deep, and made of solid iron and nickel?

317. What is the name of the 30 rigid pieces making up the Earth's surface: plates or faults?

318. What is the name of the explanation that involves the movement of the plates that make up the Earth's outer layer: plate tectonics or plate faults?

319. What are the plates called that are moving *toward* each other: convergent or divergent?

320. What are the plates called that are gradually pulling *apart*: convergent or divergent?

321. What is the name of the **theory** proposed by the German scientist *Alfred Wegener* that the continents started as one huge land mass before moving apart: continental divergence or continental drift?

322. What is the name of the ***boundary line*** where two plates meet in the Earth's crust: a slip or a fault?

323. What part of the Earth's crust moves when the magma inside the Earth moves: the tectonic plates or the fault lines?

324. What is the name of the ***fault*** under San Francisco, California: the San Francisco Fault or the San Andreas Fault?

325. What is the name of the violent shaking of the Earth's crust that most often occurs along the Earth's tectonic plates and along the fault lines?

326. What is the name of the *released energy* that travels out in waves and causes the Earth to shake as a result of an earthquake or a volcano: seismic waves or tectonic waves?

327. What is the name of the *center point* underground where most earthquakes start: the focus or the epicenter?

328. What is the name of the point on the surface of the Earth directly *above* an Earthquake's focus point where most of the violent shaking is felt: the seismic center or the epicenter?

329. What is the name for the scientists who study earthquakes: geologists or seismologists?

330. What is the name of the machine that geologists use to record the vibrations of earthquakes: a seismograph or a Richter scale?

331. What is the name given for the strength of an earthquake: intensity or magnitude?

332. What is the name of the scale that geologists use to chart the strength of an earthquake: the Seismograph scale or the Richter scale?

333. What is the powerful wave called caused by the energy of an earthquake that occurs on the ocean floor: a tidal wave or a tsunami?

334. Do *tsunami* waves start out long and low and become bigger and higher once they reach the shore?

335. What other force of nature may take place in a mountainous area, caused by an earthquake: an avalanche or a mudslide?

336. What is it called when heavy rain or an earthquake cause loose soil and rocks to slide down a mountain slope: a mudslide or a landslide?

337. What is it called when there is a slide on wet soil, and that soil becomes unstable: a mudslide or a landslide?

338. What is it called when snow becomes unstable on a mountain, breaks free, and slides down the mountain slope: an avalanche or a snow slide?

339. What is the name of the opening in the Earth's crust where gas, molten rock and ash is forced up to the surface of the earth erupting though a hole?

340. What is the name of the molten rock that flows out of the volcano when it erupts: magma or lava?

341. Where do most volcanoes occur: along the edges or along the interior of the Earth's tectonic plates?

342. What do ash and rock that spew from the opening in the Earth and pile up over time eventually harden into: mountains or rock quarries?

343. What is the name of a volcano that is erupting or is expected to erupt: active or dormant?

344. What is the name of a volcano that has not erupted for a while: active or dormant?

345. What was the name of the volcano that erupted in A.D. 79 on the western coast of Italy that buried the ancient Roman city of *Pompeii* in ash, killing over 20,000 people: Mount Vesuvius or Mount Saint Helens?

346. What is the name of the volcano that erupted in *Washington* in 1980 in which 230 square miles of forest were blown down or burned: Mount Olympus or Mount Saint Helens?

347. What is the name given to the hot water that bubbles up to the surface and forms a pond or steam: a hot spring or a geyser?

348. What is the name given to what forms when water collects in an underground cave and forces hot water to shoot up into the air: a hot spring or a geyser?

349. What is the name of the famous geyser in **Yellowstone National Park** in Wyoming that erupts regularly, sending water and steam 160 feet into the air: Old Faithful or Old Steamboat?

350. What was the name given to the continents that were crowded together into **one** landmass over 100 million years ago, gradually breaking into the continents we know today: Pangaea or Europa?

351. What is the term for the changes in the continents and their drift away from each other, a few inches per year due to plate tectonics: continental drift or continental divide?

352. How many categories of mountains are there, based on how they were formed: 3 or 4?

353. What category of mountains are the **Black Hills** of South Dakota and the **Adirondacks** of New York, the result of the uplifting of tectonic plates: dome or folded?

354. What category of mountains are the **Alps** in Europe, the **Appalachians** in the eastern United States, and the **Rocky Mountains** in western North America, the result of inter-continental plate collisions: dome or folded?

355. What category of mountains are the **Himalayas**, the Earth's tallest mountains and include *Mount Everest* that were formed over 45 million years ago: dome or folded?

356. What category of mountains are the **Grand Tetons** in the western United States, and the **Sierra Nevada** mountains in California and Nevada, the result of a combination of tension and uplift forces: fault-block mountains or tectonic dome mountains?

357. What are mountains made of: minerals or rocks?

358. What are rocks made of: minerals or elements?

359. How are rocks classified: according to how they were formed, or what they are made of?

360. How many classifications of rock are there: 3 or 5?

361. Are the three main classifications of rocks igneous, sedimentary, and metamorphic?

362. What type of rock started as hot magma and cooled into rock, and include granite, pumice, and obsidian: igneous or sedimentary?

363. Is magma another term for lava?

364. What type of **rocks** were formed when layer upon layer of debris and sand settled together, and include sandstone and limestone: sedimentary or metamorphic?

365. What type of **rocks** have changed form over time through heat and pressure, and include marble and slate: metamorphic or sedimentary?

366. Do processes that may *change* the surface of the Earth include weathering and erosion?

367. What is the process called in which water, wind, plants, and ice take boulders and turn them into rocks, then pebbles, then sand, and finally into small particles that become part of the Earth's soil: physical weathering or erosion?

368. What is the process called in which rocks weather after coming into contact with certain gases or plants, which results in an acid that can eat away at the surface of rocks: erosion or chemical weathering?

369. What is the process called in which water, rocks, and soil are constantly sliding down Earth's hills and mountains due to gravity: weathering or erosion?

370. What is the name for the layer of soil which contains small pieces of weathered rock mixed with decaying plant and animal matter called humus, replenishes itself every year, and is darker than the rest: subsoil or topsoil?

371. What is the name of the *second* layer down, is made of weathered clay and rock, and takes hundreds of thousands of years to form: bedrock or subsoil?

372. What is the name of the layer *under* the subsoil that is too far down to weather into the soil, and is made of solid rock: bedrock or sedimentary rock?

373. Do wind and ice act like ice carvers?

374. What is the name for the *slow-moving* masses of snow that have gradually compressed into ice, found in very cold regions like Antarctica, Greenland, Canada, and Alaska?

375. What it the name of the time that lasted more than a million and a half years when huge glaciers covered much of North America, northern Asia, and northern Europe: the Ice Age or the Frozen Era?

376. What did some of the water-filled, glacier-made holes become after the glaciers melted at the end of the Ice Age: Great Lakes, oceans, or rivers?

377. Are *Huron, Ontario, Michigan, Eric*, and *Superior* considered Great Lakes or Great Rivers?

378. Are *Portage, Hubbard*, and *Franz Josef* all examples of lakes or glaciers?

379. Where is *Glacier National Park* located: Montana or Wyoming?

380. Where is *Glacier **Bay** National Park* located: Alaska or Montana?

381. What is the weather like today?

382. What is the study of weather called: meteorology or astronomy?

383. What is weather the study of: the atmosphere or the environment?

384. What is the term for the layers of air that wrap around the Earth: the atmosphere or the ozone?

385. How many *major* layers of air is the Earth's atmosphere made of: 3, 4, or 5?

386. Do the five layers of the Earth's atmosphere include the troposphere, the stratosphere, the mesosphere, and thermosphere, and the exosphere?

387. What is the name of the *outermost* layer 6,000 miles beyond the Earth where the atmosphere is extremely thin and extends into space: stratosphere or exosphere?

388. What is the name of the *closest* layer to the Earth's atmosphere where all living things are found, where airplanes fly, and where the weather occurs: troposphere or mesosphere?

389. What is the name of the layer in the stratosphere that contains the gas that protects us from ultraviolet radiation from the Sun?

390. What is the name of the *coldest* layer found thirty to fifty miles above the Earth that acts as a shield, burning up meteors before they reach the Earth: thermosphere or mesosphere?

391. What is the general term that includes rain, snow, and hail and is a part of the water cycle: precipitation or weather?

392. What is the term for the **movement of water** between the surface of Earth and the atmosphere, whereby evaporated water becomes water vapor, rises to reach cooler air, condenses into tiny water droplets in the clouds, is blown across the sky by the wind, and then falls to Earth as rain: the rain cycle, the water cycle, or the life cycle?

393. What is the term for the large droplets of water that fall to the Earth?

394. What is formed on the ground and the grass when water vapor *condenses* as drops of water: dew or frost?

395. What is formed when the water vapor in the air condenses and causes a *ground-level* cloud close to the Earth's surface: fog or dew?

396. What do raindrops become when they *freeze* into lumps before they hit the ground?

397. What is formed when tiny droplets in the clouds freeze to form ice crystals and then fall to the Earth?

398. What is formed on windows and trees when the water vapor near the ground freezes into ice crystals?

399. What is the term for the measure of how hot or cold the air is?

400. What instrument do we use to measure the temperature?

401. What is the *metric term* for the measurement of temperature?

402. What is the *American term* used for the measurement of temperature?

403. What is the weather term given that refers to the distance at which things can be seen clearly: visibility or density?

404. Can fog, mist, or rain affect visibility?

405. What is the likely result when there is an *overflow* of water on land that is normally dry, affecting people, crops, and buildings?

406. What is the likely result when there is *not enough* rainwater for crops, plants, or animals for an extended period of time?

407. What is the measure of the amount of *heat energy* in the air: humidity or temperature?

408. What is the term for the amount of *moisture* in the air, humidity or temperature?

409. What is *air pressure* caused by: wind direction, or the weight of the air pushing down?

410. Which air is denser and exerts greater air pressure: hot air or cold air?

411. What are air balloons filled with to make them fly: hot air or cold air?

412. Would polar air and arctic air be considered a cold air mass or a warm air mass?

413. Would a tropical air mass be cold or warm?

414. What are the big areas of air called that circulate around the Earth: air pockets or air masses?

415. What is the term for the downward air current that may cause an aircraft to experience an abrupt change in altitude: air mass or air pocket?

416. What type of system is a mass of cool, dry air that usually brings fair weather and light winds: high pressure or low pressure?

417. What type of system is a mass of warm, moist air that usually brings stormy weather and heavy winds: high pressure or low pressure?

418. What is the *boundary* called between masses of air with different densities that is usually caused by differences in temperature: a storm or a front?

419. What kind of weather front would bring a steady rain followed by warmer temperatures: a cold front or a warm front?

420. What kind of weather front would bring a short period of heavy rain followed by clear colder weather: a cold front or a warm front?

421. What kind of front occurs when a warm air mass pushes out a cold air mass?

422. What kind of front occurs when a cold air mass pushes out a warm air mass?

423. Can the Earth's temperature be influenced by the clouds?

424. What is the name of the cloud that is made of ice crystals and are high, feathery, wispy, and thin: stratus, cirrus, or cumulus?

425. What is the name of the cloud that is white and puffy, look like cotton balls, and usually mean fair weather: stratus, cirrus, or cumulus?

426. What is the name of the cloud that looks like a grey blanket over the sky and often brings drizzle or a steady rain: stratus, cirrus, or cumulus?

427. What is the name of the clouds that get larger and darker on the bottom and often bring thunderstorms or tornados: cumulus or cumulonimbus?

428. What is the term for the huge, dark clouds called that signal the approach of a storm: thunderheads or tornadoes?

429. What is the name of the powerful white flash of electrical current that is created when the negative electrons from the cloud interact with the positive electrons of the Earth?

430. What is the name of the loud sound that is created by the lightning bolt because after the electric current is released, the air around it expands and vibrates?

431. How fast does a lightning bolt travel to our eyes: 186,000 miles per second or 1.8 million miles per second?

432. What is the name of the weather instrument that measures *air pressure*: a barometer or a hygrometer?

433. What is the name of the weather instrument that measures the *amount of moisture in* the air: a barometer or a hygrometer?

434. What is the name of the weather instrument that measures *precipitation*: a rain gauge or a hygrometer?

435. What is term for the natural movement or air across the surface of the Earth?

436. What does the continual exchange of cool and warm air create: wind or rain?

437. What is the term for wind that blows at 10 or 20 miles per hour: a breeze, a gale, or a hurricane?

438. What is the term for wind that gusts up to 40 or 50 miles per hour: a breeze, a gale, or a hurricane?

439. What is the term for the tropical cyclone that is characterized by strong winds that can travel more than 75 miles per hour; a breeze, a gale, or a hurricane?

440. Are hurricanes, typhoons, and tropical cycles all the same kind of storm, but called different names in different regions?

441. What is the name of the storm that forms a whirling, funnel-shaped cloud that reaches the surface of the Earth, and powerfully sucks up everything in its path?

442. What is the name of the storm that forms over tropical oceans in low pressure areas: a hurricane or a tsunami?

443. What is the name given to the **center** of the hurricane spiral where the air pressure is low and the winds are calm: the epicenter or the eye?

444. What is the name of the weather instrument that measures *wind speed* whereby the faster it spins, the faster the wind: a barometer or an anemometer?

445. What is the name given to the *wind pattern* in tropical areas that continues its movement in the same direction and shapes big weather patterns: prevailing winds or directional winds?

446. What is another term for *prevailing* winds: trade winds or jet stream?

447. What is it called when winds are forced to the right North of the equator and forced to the left South of the equator, due to the Earth's rotation: Coriolis Effect or Trade Winds?

448. What is the name for the fast-moving air current high in the Earth's atmosphere: a jet stream or a trade wind?

449. What kind of ocean waves are caused by high winds?

450. What kind of storm can high winds whip up in a desert?

451. What is the name for the fierce snowstorm with high winds that occurs when cold, Arctic air mixes with warm, moist air?

452. What is the name for the average weather pattern that includes the latitude, temperature, rainfall, snowfall, and humidity in a particular area: a zone or a climate?

453. What would tropical, desert, semiarid, subtropical, tundra, polar, and highland all be considered on the Earth?

454. What is the name of the climate that occurs near the equator characterized by high temperatures and high humidity: polar or tropical?

455. What is the name of the climate that occurs near the North and South Poles where the temperatures are cold: polar or tundra?

456. What changes for plants, animals, and humans depending on the climate they live in: habitat or weather?

457. Have people, animals, and plants adapted to the climate in which they live?

458. What natural division of the year is determined by the changing position of the Earth in relation to the Sun, and what part of the Earth is tilted toward the Sun?

459. In regions that have four seasons, is the weather different in each of those seasons?

460. What imaginary line divides the Northern Hemisphere and the Southern Hemispheres?

461. Are the seasons the same or the opposite in the Northern and Southern Hemispheres?

462. Is the date on the calendar the same or different in the Northern and Southern Hemispheres?

463. What is the first day of summer in the Northern hemisphere: June 21st or September 21st?

464. What season is it in the Southern Hemisphere beginning on June 21st?

465. What is the first day of autumn in the Northern Hemisphere: June 21st or September 21st?

466. What is the first day of winter in the Northern Hemisphere: September 21st or December 21st?

467. What is the first day of spring in the Northern Hemisphere: March 21st or September 21st?

468. What season is it in the Southern Hemisphere beginning on March 21st?

469. Do some regions near the equator where the temperature does not vary too much have wet and dry seasons based on variations in rainfall?

470. What is the name of the wind in southern Asia that create the wet and dry seasons: monsoon or typhoon?

471. What is the name of a tropical cyclone in the South Pacific: monsoon or typhoon?

472. What kind of weather do you like best?

473. What kind of climate would you most like to live in?

474. What is the study of the **body structures** of a human: anatomy or biology?

475. What body parts can you name that are *outside* the human body?

476. What body parts can you name that are *inside* the human body?

477. What is the name of the structural part of a body system that is composed of tissues that allow it to perform a specific function: an organ or a muscle?

478. What is the *largest* organ in or on your body: your stomach or your skin?

479. What is the name of the organ that is part of the body's *circulatory system* that pumps blood through your body: the heart or the lungs?

480. Is the heart organ a muscle?

481. How many *chambers* is the heart divided into?

482. What is the name for the top two chambers of the heart: atria or ventricles?

483. What is the name of the bottom two chambers of the heart: atria or ventricles?

484. How many *valves* does the human heart have: 4 or 8?

485. What allows the ventricles and atria to open and close, allowing blood to flow through the heart: arteries or valves?

486. What is the name of the *largest artery* in the human body that branches out to take the blood to all parts of the body: the aorta or the vein?

487. What is the term for the hollow, stretchy tubes that transport the blood through your body: blood vessels or capillaries?

488. What is the name of the blood vessels that carry oxygen-rich blood *away* from your heart: capillaries or arteries?

489. What is the name of the blood vessels that carry blood *back* to your heart for more oxygen: arteries or veins?

490. What is the name for the *smaller* blood vessels delivering oxygen and nutrients that branch out and connect the veins and arteries, bringing blood in contact with the cells of the body: ventricles or capillaries?

491. What is the term for the pushing force that moves the blood through the body caused by the pumping of the heart: pulse or blood pressure?

492. What on your body indicates how often our heart squeezes to pump blood throughout your body: pulse or blood pressure?

493. How many pulses per minute is the average human heart rate per minute but varies from person to person: 30 or 60?

494. Does your heart rate go up or down when you exercise, because your cells lose oxygen and need more?

495. What delivers nutrients from food and oxygen to the cells in organs, nerves, muscles, and bones: blood or platelets?

496. What gas do you release when you breathe out, that blood carries back to your lungs: oxygen or carbon dioxide?

497. What is the name of the part of the blood that is a clear, thin liquid: hemoglobin or plasma?

498. What are the two *colors* of blood cells that float in the plasma?

499. What is the name of the substance in red blood cells that carries oxygen and carbon dioxide: hemoglobin or platelets?

500. What blood cells in your body travel in the blood and help fight disease and infection: red or white?

501. What is the name for the tiny solids in the blood that make blood coagulate or get thinker to help stop bleeding: hemoglobin or platelets?

502. How long is it before new red blood cells *replace* old blood cells: four weeks or four months?

503. What is the rate at which your red blood cells die: 8 million per second or 2 million per second?

504. What organ in your body helps remove dead blood cells by breaking them down and reusing what it can as nutrients: spleen or liver?

505. What organ in your body is the cleansing organ, and helps you filter your blood and removes harmful wastes: spleen or liver?

506. What did the English doctor **William Harvey** theorize was the center of the circulatory system: the heart or the lungs?

507. What may be the result when the heart does not receive enough oxygen and heart muscle cells die?

508. What substance if eaten to excess can lead to a build-up on the inside of arteries that may lead to a heart attack: sugars or saturated fats?

509. What is another name for a heart attack: cardiac arrest or coronary arrest?

510. What is it called when a person receives blood from another person: a transfusion or a blood transfer?

511. How many types of blood did an Austrian doctor conclude that there are back in 1900: three or four?

512. What are **A, B, AB**, and **0** regarded as, based on the protein contained in the red blood cells?

513. What is the name of the factor that indicates whether a blood type is positive or negative: the **Rh** factor or the **Ra** factor?

514. What is the most common blood type and is considered the *"universal donor:"* Type **A** or Type **O**?

515. Which **Rh** factor do 85% of Americans have: positive or negative?

516. Can a patient receiving a blood transfusion receive any type of blood, or does the patient need to receive a blood type that is compatible with the patient's own blood type?

517. What may be the effect if a patient receives a blood type that is not compatible with the patient's own blood type: blood clots or hardened arteries?

518. Is your blood type inherited just like your eye color?

519. Do you know *your* blood type?

520. Do different animals have the same or different blood types?

521. Are certain blood types more common than others in different countries?

522. What system is *blood* a function of: respiratory or circulatory?

523. What system is breathing a function of: respiratory or circulatory?

524. How many times a day does the average person breathe in and out: 5,000 or 20,000?

525. What system is your lungs part of: circulatory or respiratory?

526. What is the name for the two inflatable sacs that expand and contract to help you breathe and are located on either side of your heart: lungs or kidneys?

527. What part of your body does your air flow down when you take a breath through your nose or mouth: trachea, or bronchi?

528. What is the term for the tubes inside your lungs: air sacs or bronchial tubes?

529. What is the term for the air sacs at the ends of the bronchi that contain small capillaries where the circulatory and respiratory systems meet: alveoli or diaphragm?

530. What is the term for the piece of muscle underneath your lungs that arches down to allow air in, and arches down forcing air out through the windpipe: the air sacs or the diaphragm?

531. What can cause a person's lungs to clog with tar, cause lung cancer, and place a strain on the heart and lungs forcing them to work harder and less effectively?

532. What things do you do to keep your body healthy?

CHAPTER 5

Math - 4th Grade

1. What place value comes after 1?

2. How many zeros are in the number 10?

3. What place value comes after ten?

4. How many zeros are in the number 100?

5. What place value comes after one hundred?

6. How many zeros are in the number 1,000?

7. What place value comes after one thousand?

8. How many zeros are in the number 10,000?

9. What place value comes after ten thousand?

10. How many zeros are in the number 100,000?

11. What place value comes after one hundred thousand?

12. How many zeros are there in 1,000,000?

13. What place value comes after one million?

14. What place value comes after ten million?

15. What place value comes after one hundred million?

16. What is the next highest number place value after one thousand billion: one trillion or one quadrillion?

17. What can you name that can be measured in the billions?

18. If you write numbers larger than ten thousand, what symbol might you write to show the correct place value?

19. Moving right to left, how many digits do you count before inserting a comma?

20. How would you read the number one comma, two three four comma, five six seven?

21. Do you **have to** use a comma for a number between one thousand and nine thousand nine hundred and ninety-nine?

22. Is "three comma one two three" the same as "three one two three" with no comma?

23. How many zeros are there in 1000?

24. How many zeros are there in 100,000?

25. How many zeros are there in one million?

26. How many zeros are there in 10,000?

27. In the decimal system, what number are the place values based on?

28. What do we call the time span of **ten** years?

29. What do we call the time span of **100** years?

30. How is the number *"one hundred thousand five hundred"* written in standard form?

31. How is 8,243 written in expanded form?

32. Using digits how would you write the number five thousand forty?

33. Are numbers to the right of 0 on a number line positive or negative numbers?

34. Are numbers to the left of 0 on a number line positive or negative numbers?

35. Is 75-15 an odd or even number?

36. Is the difference of 50-9 an odd or even number?

37. Are negative numbers similar to having debt, or being in the "red?"

38. Are positive number similar to showing a profit, or being in the "black?"

39. Are the numerals zero through nine considered Arabic or Roman?

40. Can you write the letters of the Roman numerals one through five?

41. Can you write the letters of the Roman numerals six through ten?

42. What Arabic number is the letter **L** equal to: 50 or 100?

43. What Arabic number is the letter **C** equal to: 100 or 1,000?

44. What Arabic number is the letter **D** equal to: 500 or 1,000?

45. What Arabic number is the letter **M** equal to: 10,000 or 1,000?

46. If smaller Roman numerals are on the left of a larger number, do we add or subtract that value?

47. What is **XL** as an Arabic number?

48. If smaller Roman numerals are on the right of a larger number, do we add or subtract that value?

49. What is **LX** as an Arabic number?

50. In Roman numerals if **M**=1000 and **C**=100 and **L**=50, what is **MCL** equal to?

51. What is Roman numeral **XVIII** equal to?

52. How would you write the year **2021** as a Roman numeral?

53. Do some clocks have Roman numerals?

54. What is the rule for rounding a number if it is four or less: round up or down to the nearest ten?

55. What is the rule for rounding a number if it is five or more: round up or down to the nearest ten?

56. What is 2,500 rounded to the nearest thousand?

57. What is 2,200 rounded to the nearest thousand?

58. What is 2,890 rounded to the nearest hundred?

59. What is 2,255 rounded to the nearest ten?

60. What is the name of a number that can only be divided by itself and by the number one: a prime number or a composite number?

61. What is the name of a number that can be divided by at least one other number: a prime number or a composite number?

62. If a number has only two factors, is it called a prime number or a composite number?

63. Are zero and one prime numbers?

64. What kind of numbers are 2, 3, 5, 7, 11, 13, and 17: prime numbers or composite numbers?

65. What kind of numbers are 1, 2, 3, 6, 9, and 12: prime numbers or composite numbers?

66. Is 28 a prime or composite number?

67. Is 59 a prime or composite number?

68. Can you add numbers up to one million?

69. What is 50,000 plus 90,000?

70. What do nine hundred thousand plus one hundred thousand equal?

71. What is the **sum** of six thousand, plus three hundred, plus fifty- two?

72. What addition property is 1 + (2 + 3) in parenthesis = (1 + 2) in parenthesis + 3 an example of: the distributive or the associative?

73. What addition property is 1 + 2= 2 + 1 an example of: the identity or the commutative?

74. What addition property is 1 + 0 =1 an example of: the identity, distributive, or the associative?

75. What is the approximate sum if you round to the nearest thousand and then add the following numbers together: 4,100 + 3,987?

76. Can you subtract numbers up to one million?

77. Do you know how to borrow from the higher place value when subtracting numbers?

78. What is 185,000 – 84,000?

79. What is 180,000 – 15,000?

80. What is 1,000,000 – 650,000?

81. Can you estimate the difference of 780 - 314?

82. Do you know your multiplication facts up to 10 x 10?

83. In the equation 3 x 8 = 24, which numbers are the factors?

84. In the equation 2 x 8 = 24, which number is the product?

85. What are some multiples of the number 2?

86. What are some multiples of the number 6?

87.   What is the number 28 a multiple of?

88.   What is the number 81 a multiple of?

89.   What **two** numbers is 18 a multiple of?

90.   Is the number 96 a multiple of 12 or 14?

91.   What is it called when you take a number and multiply it by itself: a square or a multiplier?

92.   Is 4 x 4 = 16 the same as saying 4 squared equals 16?

93.   What is 2 x 2?

94.   What is 5 x 5?

95.   What is 6 x 6?

96.   What is 7 x 7?

97.   What is 8 x 8?

98.   What is 9 x 9?

99.   What is 10 x 10?

100. What is the square root of 4?

101. What is the square root of 36, or what number when multiplied by itself equals 36?

102. What is the square root of 25?

103. What is the square root of 81?

104. What is the square root of 49?

105. What is the square root of 121?

106. What is the square root of 64?

107. What is the square root of 144?

108. What is the product of 3 x 4 x 2?

109. When you are multiplying numbers by ten, what number do you add to the number that you are multiplying by: 0 or 1?

110. What is the product of 44 x 10?

111. What is the product of 220 x 10?

112. Can you multiply by tens, hundreds, and thousands?

113. What is a little trick you can use when multiplying numbers ending in zeros like 200 x 400?

114. How many zeros would you add to find the product of 200 x 400?

115. What is the product of 200 x 400: 8,000 or 80,000?

116. What property is 1 x 5 = 5 an example of: the associative, distributive, identity, or zero property of multiplication?

117. What property is 3 x (4-3) in parenthesis = 3 x 4 – 3 x 3 an example of: the associative, distributive, identity, or zero property of multiplication?

118. What property is (1 x 3) in parenthesis x 4 = 1 x (3 x 4) in parenthesis an example of: the associative, distributive, identity, or zero property of multiplication?

119. What property is 28 x 0 an example of: the associative, distributive, identity, or zero property of multiplication?

120. What property is 22 x 1 and example of: the associative, distributive, identity or zero property of multiplication?

121. How would you estimate the product of 4 x 3,120 rounding to the nearest thousand?

122. What is the product of 7000 x 10 using the trick with adding the zeros?

123. Is 2 x 8 greater than, less than, or equal to 15?

124. Is 2 x 9 greater than, less than, or equal to 18?

125. Is 5 x 8 greater than, less than, or equal to 45?

126. What is the inverse operation of multiplication: division or addition?

127. How would you invert the equation 10 x 2 = 20?

128. How would you invert the equation 24 ÷ 8 = 3?

129. What number is the *dividend* in the equation: 20 ÷ 5 = 4?

130. What number is the *divisor* in the equation: 20 ÷ 5 = 4?

131. What number is the *quotient* in the equation: 20 ÷ 5 = 4?

132. What is the quotient of the problem: 72 ÷ 8?

133. In the equation 12 ÷ 3 = 4, what does number 12 represent: the divisor or the dividend?

134. In the equation 12 ÷ 3 = 4, what does number 4 represent: the quotient or the divisor?

135. In the equation 12 ÷ 3 = 4, what does the number 3 represent: the divisor or the dividend?

136. In the equation 20 ÷ 1 = 20, what number is both the quotient and the dividend?

137. Do you remember your division facts up to 12?

138. What is any number divided by 1 equal to?

139. What is the product of an equation where a number is divided by itself?

140. How would you write 12 ÷ 3 as a fraction?

141. If there are 16 people in line for the rollercoaster and each car holds four people, how many cars will they fill up?

142. What is a number called that divides another number evenly and does not have a remainder: a factor or a prime number?

143. If 4 ÷4 =1, 4 ÷ 2 = 2, and 4 ÷1 = 1, what are the *factors* of 4?

144. What are the factors of 24?

145. What common factors do the numbers 20 and 24 have?

146. If Brandon has 7 cookies and he wants to divide them equally among 3 lunch boxes, how many would there be left over for him to eat? (7 ÷ 3 = __ R __)

147. What is 26 ÷ 6?

148. What is 246 ÷ 2?

149. What is 246 ÷ 3? (24 ÷3=__, 6 ÷3=__)

150. What is 963 ÷ 3? (9 ÷3=__, 6 ÷ 3=__, 3 ÷ 3=__)

151. What is a related multiplication fact for 24 ÷ 8 = 3?

152. What is 180 ÷ 3?

153. What is 6000 ÷ 100?

154. What is 83 ÷ 10? __Remainder ___

155. Is 21 ÷ 3 greater than, less than, or equal to 8?

156. Is 24 ÷ 8 greater than, less than, or equal to 2?

157. Is 32 ÷ 4 greater than, less than, or equal to 6?

158. Can you divide bigger numbers on paper using long division?

159. What is the type of math called in which letters and symbols are used to represent an unknown number?

160. What is the value of **a + 5** if **a** = 15?

161. Using the order of operations and doing what is in parenthesis first, how would you simplify the following equation: 8÷(4 ÷ 2) in parenthesis, + 3?

162. How would you solve for **a** if: **a** x 5 = 30? (**a** = __)

163. Are you able to read a graph and coordinates?

164. Are you able to read and interpret data on tables, lines, and graphs?

165. What is the missing number in the pattern: 1, 3, 6, 12, __?

166. What is the missing number in the pattern: 1, 2, __, 8, 16?

167. What is the next number in the sequence: 1, 3, 6, 10, __?

168. What is the name of the *currency* that we use in the United States?

169. Can you name some currencies that are used in *other* countries?

170. Can you describe the symbol we use for the **dollar**?

171. Can you describe the symbol we use for **cents**?

172. Which has a higher value: four quarters or $1.25?

173. Which has the highest value: two twenty-dollar bills; a ten, and a five; or a fifty-dollar bill?

174. What would $489 be rounded to the nearest ten?

175. What would $489 be rounded to the nearest 100?

176. What would $29.99 be rounded to the nearest ten?

177. When we make purchases, do we have of allow extra for tax in our state?

178. What is the total of 25 cents plus 50 cents plus 10 cents?

179. If Jake raised $22, Megan raised $12, and Cole raised $11 selling raffle tickets, how much money did they raise all together?

180. If you and two friends just bought a pizza for $21.00 and you divided the cost evenly, how much would each of you pay?

181. How much change did Erin receive if she bought a bag of apples for $4.49 and she paid with a ten-dollar bill? (Round 49 to __, subtract from 10.)

182. How much would Brianna pay if she bought 4 notebooks that cost 2 dollars each?

183. How much would Spencer pay if he bought 2 packs of baseball cards that cost $2.40 each?

184. What is the *unit price* of undershirts if a 3-pack costs $12.00?

185. Which President is on the front of a **one-dollar** bill: George Washington or Abraham Lincoln?

186. Which President is on the front of a **five-dollar** bill: George Washington or Abraham Lincoln?

187. Which President is on the front of a **ten-dollar** bill: Alexander Hamilton or Abraham Lincoln?

188. Which President is on the front of a **twenty-dollar** bill: Alexander Hamilton or Andrew Jackson?

189. Which President is on the front of a **fifty-dollar** bill: Ulysses S. Grant or Alexander Hamilton?

190. Which President is on the front of a **penny**: George Washington or Abraham Lincoln?

191. Which President is on the front of a **nickel**: Abraham Lincoln or Thomas Jefferson?

192. Which President is on the front of a **dime**: Franklin D. Roosevelt or Harry Truman?

193. Who is the president on the front of a **quarter**: George Washington or Abraham Lincoln?

194. What are the units of *time,* smallest to largest, starting with seconds and going up to one year?

195. How many days are equal to one year?

196. How do we accommodate the extra ¼ day that we have each year?

197. If there are 365 days in one year, how many days are in ½ year?

198. How many hours are there in one day?

199. How many hours are there in ½ a day?

200. How many hours are there in ¼ of a day?

201. How many hours are there in ¾ of a day?

202. How many seconds are there in one minute?

203. How many minutes are there in one hour?

204. How many hours would 90 minutes be equal to?

205. How many minutes in ½ hour?

206. How many minutes in ¼ hour?

207. How many minutes would 5 quarter hours be equal to?

208. How many minutes would there be in 3 hours and 12 minutes? (3 x 60 + 12)

209. How many minutes and seconds would there be in 124 seconds? (2 x 60 + 4)

210. How many minutes are there in 2 ¼ hours? (2 x 60 + 15)

211. If you went two camp for 3 weeks, how many days would you be there?

212. What do **"Pacific, Mountain, Central**, and **Eastern"** refer to with regard to time?

213. What is the name of the time zone that you live in?

214. Are television shows on at different times, depending on the time zone they are broadcast in?

215. If it is now 8:25, what time will it be in one hour?

216. What is another way of saying 9:40?

217. If Callie started her test at 1:45 and finished 40 minutes later, what time did she finish?

218. If the bus trip to Boston is 8 ½ hours long and it leaves at 10:00 a.m., what time will arrive at its destination?

219. Do you know how to read a transportation schedule in an airport or a train station?

220. What measurement system is used in the United States: the metric system or U.S. customary units?

221. What are the U.S. customary units of measurements smallest to largest starting with inches?

222. How many inches are in one foot?

223. What fractions of an inch are also indicated on a ruler or measuring instrument?

224. What can we do to approximate the measurement of something?

225. How many feet are in one yard?

226. How many feet are in 1 and 1/3 yards?

227. How many inches are in one yard?

228. How many inches are in a ½ yard?

229. What customary unit is 5,280 feet long?

230. If 5,280 feet equals one mile, how many feet are there in ½ mile?

231. What customary unit has 1760 yards: a mile or a kilometer?

232. What is the sum of 2 feet 6 inches plus 3 feet 6 inches?

233. What are the U.S. customary units of weight smallest to largest starting with ounces?

234. How many ounces are there in 1 pound: 16 or 24?

235. How many ounces are there in ½ pound?

236. How many ounces are there in ¾ pound?

237. How many ounces are there in 2 pounds?

238. What customary unit do we often use to estimate weight: pounds or ounces?

239. How many pounds would 48 ounces be equal to?

240. What is the abbreviation of ounce?

241. What is the abbreviation of pound?

242. How many pounds equal one ton: 2000 or 3000?

243. What U.S. customary unit would 6,000 pounds be equal to?

244. What is the abbreviation for ton: t or tn?

245. If a truck weighs 3 ½ tons, how many pounds does it weigh?

246. What are the U.S. customary units for volume, smallest to largest, starting with one cup?

247. What are the U.S. customary units of cooking, smallest to largest, starting with the teaspoon?

248. How many teaspoons are equal to one tablespoon?

249. What is the abbreviation for teaspoon?

250. What is the abbreviation for tablespoon?

251. How many fluid ounces are equal to 1 cup: 4 or 8?

252. What is the abbreviation in a recipe for cup?

253. When we measure volume when we cook, what are the common sizes of cups?

254. How many fluid ounces are equal to one cup: 8 or 16?

255. How many cups are there in one pint: 2 or 4?

256. What is the abbreviation for pint?

257. How many pints are there in one quart: ½ or 2?

258. What is the abbreviation for quart?

259. How many quarts are there in one gallon: 2 or 4?

260. Which is larger: 3 pints or 4 cups?

261. How many tablespoons are equal to 3 tablespoons and 1 teaspoon?

262. What unit of measurement is used in many other countries?

263. What system meaning "ten" is the Metric system based on?

264. What number is associated with **dec**imal, **dec**agon, and **dec**ade?

265. What number is associated with **cen**timeter, **cen**tipede, **cen**tury, and **cen**tennial?

266. What number is associated with **mil**limeter, **mil**lipede, and **mil**lennium?

267. How many millimeters equals one centimeter: 100 or 10?

268. If a caterpillar is 32 millimeters long, how long is it in centimeters?

269. What is the abbreviation for centimeter?

270. What is the abbreviation for millimeter?

271. How many centimeters are equal to one meter: 100 or 1000?

272. What is the abbreviation for meter?

273. Which is longer: a meter or a yard?

274. How many meters are there in one kilometer: 100 or 1000?

275. What is the abbreviation for kilometer?

276. Which is longer: a kilometer or a mile?

277. How many miles is 100 kilometers equal to: 620 or 62?

278. What is the metric unit for measuring liquid capacity: liter or gram?

279. How many centiliters are there in one liter: 10 or 100?

280. How many milliliters are there in one liter: 100 or 1000?

281. What is the abbreviation for centiliters?

282. What is the abbreviation for liter?

283. If you and a friend had a one-liter bottle of chocolate milk, and you both drank half of it, how many milliliters would you have left: 500 or 1000?

284. What are the metric units of weight smallest to largest: the gram, kilogram, milligram and metric ton?

285. How many grams are equal to one kilogram: 100 or 1000?

286. How many milligrams are there in one centigram: 10 or 100?

287. What is the abbreviation for milligram?

288. What is the abbreviation for centigram?

289. How many milligrams are there in one gram: 100 or 1000?

290. What is the abbreviation for gram?

291. How many centigrams are there in one gram: 100 or 1000?

292. What is the abbreviation for kilogram?

293. Which unit of measurement is used to conduct most science experiments: the U.S. customary system or the metric system?

294. What is the metric unit of measurement for temperature: Celsius or Fahrenheit?

295. What is the U.S. customary unit of measurement for temperature?

296. If it is 32 degrees Fahrenheit, what is the temperature in degrees Celsius?

297. Is 0 degrees Celsius or 32 degrees Fahrenheit the temperature in which water melts or freezes?

298. What do we call the numbers that are greater than zero but less than one?

299. What is the numerator in the fraction 2/3?

300. What is the denominator in the fraction 4/10?

301. What can 2/4 be reduced to in lowest terms: ½ or ¾?

302. What is the simplest form of the fraction 4/16?

303. Are 1/3 and 3/6 equivalent fractions?

304. What is the equivalent fraction of ¾?

305. What is the equivalent fraction of 1/3?

306. Which fraction is equal to 6/10: ¾ or 3/5?

307. What fraction comes next in the pattern: ½, 2/4, 3/6, ___?

308. Is 9/6 considered a proper or an improper fraction?

309. When the numerator is the same number as the denominator, what number is that fraction equal to?

310. What kind of a fraction is it if the numerator is larger than the denominator: mixed or improper?

311. If you have the fraction 10/5, is that the same as 10 ÷ 5?

312. What is an improper fraction that can be divide evenly with no remainder equal to: a whole number or a mixed fraction?

313. What is 12/3 equal to as a whole number?

314. What whole number is 3/3 equal to?

315. What is 0/8 equal to?

316. What math operation is a bar in a fraction equal to: division or multiplication?

317. Can the fraction 4/10 be reduced?

318. Do you need to divide both the numerator and the denominator by a common factor to reduce a fraction to its lowest terms?

319. What is 4/16 in lowest terms?

320. What is 18/24 in lowest terms?

321. What do we call a number that has both a whole number and a fraction like 1 1/3: mixed or improper?

322. How can the improper fraction 12/5 be written as a mixed number? $(12 \div 5 = 2 \textbf{R2})$

323. How would you write the mixed number 6 ¼ as an improper fraction: multiply 4 x 6 plus 1 over 4, or add 6 + 1 over 4?

324. How would you write the mixed number 4 and 2/3 as an improper fraction? $(3 \times 4 + 2)$

325. What number is ½ of 12?

326. What number is 1/3 of 18?

327. What number is ¼ of 16?

328. How do we add fractions with common denominators: by adding or multiplying the numerators?

329. What is the sum of 3/5 + 1/5?

330. What is the sum of 4/9 + 8/9?

331. What is the sum of 2/10 + 3/10 + 4/10?

332. How would you write 12/9 as a mixed number in its lowest terms?

333. What is 5/7 – 3/7?

334. How do you add fractions with unlike denominators: find the least common denominator first, or simply add the original denominators together?

335. What is the sum of ½ and 1/3? $(3/6 + 2/6 = \_)$

336. How do you subtract fractions with unlike denominators: find the least common denominator first, or simply subtract the original denominators together?

337. What is ½ - 1/6 reduced to simple terms?   (3/6 – 1/6 =_)

338. What is 7/9 – 3/9?

339. If Anika and Eva picked 2 pounds of strawberries and they ate ½ pound of them, how many pounds of strawberries do they have left?

340. What is the sum of 1 and 1/3 + 1 and 1/3?

341. If Sam is 5 ½ feet tall and Jordan is 3 ½ feet tall, how much taller is Sam than Jordan?

342. If Sofia is 4 ½ feet tall and her sister Isabella is 4 feet tall, how much taller is Sofia than Isabella?

343. If Sofia is ½ foot taller than Isabella, how much taller is she is inches?

344. Is 2/5 + 1/5 greater than, less than, or equal to 4/5?

345. Is 1/3/ + 1/3 greater than, less than, or equal to 2/3?

346. Is ¼ + ¾ greater than, less than, or equal to 1?

347. When following recipes, is it a good idea to use measuring cups and measuring spoons?

348. What is the order smallest to largest of the following measuring cups: ½ 1/3, ¼, and 1?

349. What is the order smallest to largest of the following teaspoons: ¼, 1/8, ½, and 1?

350. If Sarah's class has 12 boys and 12 girls, how much of the class is made up of girls?

351. What fraction would indicate how many of the fish are blue if there are 100 tropical fish in the aquarium, 75 are gold, and 25 are blue: ½, ¼, 2/3, or ¾?

352. What is the product when you multiply the fraction ½ x 3?

353. What is the product when you multiply 2/3 x 1/3?

354. What is the product when you multiply ½ x 2/5?

355. If a candy bar costs one quarter or 25 cents, and there are four quarters in one dollar, what part of a dollar is 25 cents?

356. What fraction of a dollar is fifty cents?

357. What fraction of a dollar is 75 cents?

358. How do we indicate dollars and cents: with decimals or with commas?

359. What is $4.00 + $2.75?

360. What is $4.00 - $2.75?

361. What number is the decimal system based on?

362. What do we call the time span of ten years?

363. How would you write two dollars and fifty cents using a decimal point?

364. How is the fraction 1/10 written as a decimal?

365. How is the fraction 1/100 written as a decimal?

366. How is the fraction 1/1000 written as a decimal?

367. Is 1.2 greater than, less than, or equal to 1.20?

368. Are the decimals .9 and .90 equivalent?

369. Is .9 greater than, less than, or equal to .09?

370. How would you write the fraction two and four tenths as a decimal?

371. How would point two five be written as a fraction?

372. How would point seven five be written as a fraction?

373. How would point five zero be written as a fraction?

374. In the number 0.5, which digit is in the ones place?

375. What would 3.273 be rounded to the nearest tenth if you consider the number to the right of 2?

376. What would 4.86 be rounded to the nearest tenth if you consider the number to the right of 8?

377. What would 4.83 be rounded to the nearest tenth if you consider the number to the right of 8?

378. What would 3.263 be rounded to the nearest hundredth if you consider the number to the right of 2?

379. What would 3.457 be rounded to the nearest hundredth if you consider the number to the right of 4?

380. What would 3.248 be rounded to the nearest tenth if you consider the number to the right of 4?

381. What is 5.612 rounded to the nearest whole number?

382. Can you read decimals on a number line?

383. What decimal would come next in the sequence: 1.5, 1.6, 1.7, ___?

384. What do you have to line up when you are adding decimals together: whole numbers or decimal points?

385. What number do you need to add to 1.2 to make it line up evenly with 1.35 before you add them together?

386. Can you *estimate* the sum of the following by rounding each number to the nearest whole number, and then adding them together: 4.8 + 2.1 = ___?

387. What is the sum of 1.5 + 1.4?

388. What is the sum of 2.5 + 2.5?

389. If Andrew watched his turtle move 0.2 centimeters, then move 0.4 centimeters more, and then 0.3 centimeters more, how much distance did his turtle travel in all?

390. Is 5/4 greater than, less than, or equal to 1.25?

391. What is the study of points, lines, segments, and shapes called?

392. Which can go on infinitely: a line or a line segment?

393. What symbols are line segments often labeled with: letters or numbers?

394. What do we draw at either end of a line to show that it can go on forever in either direction?

395. What is the name of a line that has one end point and an arrow pointing in one direction: a segment or a ray?

396. What point to we start with when we are labeling a ray: the end point or the point closer to the arrow?

397. What is formed when two rays have the same end point: an angle or a line segment?

398. What is another name for the end point: the axis or the vertex?

399. How many sides does a triangle have?

400. What is the name of an angle that forms a square corner?

401. How many degrees does a right-angle measure: 45 or 90?

402. What is the name of an angle that is *less* than a right angle: acute or obtuse?

403. What is the name of an angle that is *greater* than a right angle: acute or obtuse?

404. Can we help ourselves remember the difference between *a*cute and *o*btuse if we think that "**a**" is a lower (or lesser) letter than "**o**" which is 'higher' in the alphabet?

405. What is the name of a triangle that has **two** sides that are equal: isosceles or equilateral?

406. If you have a triangle with each angle measuring 60 degrees, what kind of triangle is it: isosceles or equilateral?

407. What is the name of a triangle that has 3 sides with different lengths: isosceles or scalene?

408. If a triangle has one angle that measures 90 degrees, what kind of triangle is it: equilateral or right?

409. What is the name of the tool you can use similar to a ruler for measuring angles: a protractor or a compass?

410. If an angle measures 80 degrees and part of the angle measures 30 degrees, what is the measurement of the *adjacent* angle? (80-30= __)

411. How many degrees is ½ turn of an angle: 90 or 180?

412. How many degrees is ¼ turn of an angle: 45 or 90?

413. How many degrees is ¾ turn of an angle: 180 or 270?

414. How many degrees is 1 full turn of an angle: 270 or 360?

415. What do we call two lines when they cross each other: intersecting or parallel?

416. What do we call two lines that intersect each other and form right angles: perpendicular or parallel?

417. What do we call lines that always stay the same distance apart and never intersect: perpendicular or parallel?

418. What are lines called that run east and west like the **"horizon?"**

419. What are lines called that run up and down, or north and south?

420. What are lines called that run northeast to southwest, or join two opposite vertices of a quadrilateral?

421. What is the general term of a closed plane shape that has three or more line segments and angles: a polygon or a hexagon?

422. What is the name of a polygon that is three-sided?

423. What is the name of a polygon that has four sides: a quadrilateral or a diagonal?

424. What two quadrilateral shapes have *two* pairs of parallel lines?

425. What is the name of a quadrilateral with sides that run parallel: a parallelogram or a matrix?

426. What is a quadrilateral called that has *one* pair of parallel lines: a trapezoid or a rhombus?

427. What is a rectangle called that has four sides that are all the same exact length?

428. What is a diamond an example of: a rhombus or a trapezoid?

429. What is the name of any polygon with four sides: a square or a quadrilateral?

430. What is the name of a polygon with five sides: a pentagon or a hexagon?

431. What is the name of a polygon with six sides: a pentagon or a hexagon?

432. What is the name of the polygon with seven sides: a hexagon or a heptagon?

433. What is the name of a polygon with eight sides: a hexagon or an octagon?

434. What is the name of a polygon with nine sides: a decagon or a nonagon?

435. What is the name of a polygon with ten sides: a decagon or a pentagon?

436. What animal are you familiar with that has **8** "arms?"

437. Which polygon is the shape of a red stop sign?

438. What is the name of a polygon that has 4 straight lines of equal length, but the lines do not form right angles: a rhombus or a trapezoid?

439. What are shapes called that have the same shape and the same size: congruent or similar?

440. What are shapes called that have the same shape but are *not* the same size: congruent or similar?

441. What is a shape called that has matching points on both sides of a line dividing it, and if you folded it in half it would match up exactly: symmetrical or asymmetrical?

442. What part of a shape would a line of symmetry run through?

443. If you multiply the length times the width of a square or a rectangle, what would you be measuring: area or perimeter?

444. If a rectangle measures 8 centimeters long and 4 centimeters wide, what is its area?

445. If a square measures 3 feet by 3 feet, what is its area?

446. Do we measure area in square units?

447. If there are 12 inches in one foot, how many inches are there in 1 square foot? (12x12=___)

448. What are some examples of U.S. customary units of area besides square inch?

449. What are some examples of metric units of area besides square millimeter?

450. Are polygons 2 or 3 dimensional?

451. Can 2-dimensional shapes be drawn on a plane?

452. What is the name of the **3**-dimensional shape that often has a triangular or rectangular base, and can break light into the colors of the spectrum?

453. What is the name of the **3**-dimensional shape that has two flat circular ends and is shaped like a tube?

454. What is the name of the **3**-dimensional shape that often has a polygon base and sides that are triangular that meet to form a point at the, and is also the name of the buildings that the ancient Egyptians and Maya built?

455. What is the name of the **3**-dimensional shape that has no flat surfaces and all points of the shape are the same distance from the center of the shape, similar to a globe?

456. What is the name of the **3**-dimensional shape that has 6 square faces, similar to dice?

457. What is the name of the **3**-dimensional shape that has a base that is round and a point at the top, similar to what you crunch on under your scoop of ice cream?

458. What part of a **3**-dimensional shape includes the top, bottom, left, right, front, and back: the perimeter or the surface area?

459. Can you count the sides, edges, vertices, and faces on geometric figures?

460. When we measure the amount of space or cubic units that a 3-dimensional figure takes up, what are we measuring: the surface area or the volume?

461. If a rectangular prism has 6 cubes on one layer and there are 2 layers, how many cubic centimeters are in the prism?

462. Is a circle a polygon?

463. What is the name of the tool you can use to draw a circle: a compass or a protractor?

464. What is it called when you draw a straight line from the center of a circle to any point on the outer edge of the circle: diameter or radius?

465. What is it called when you draw a straight line from one point on the circle, through the center of the circle to the opposite end point: diameter or radius?

466. What is it called when you draw a straight line that join two points on a curve of a circle: chord or arc?

467. Which is longer: the radius or the diameter?

468. What can you adjust on a compass to determine the size of the circle: the radius or the diameter?

469. If the radius of a circle is 8 centimeters, what is its diameter: 16 or 64?

470. What is the distance around a circle called: its radius or its circumference?

471. Can you make a prediction about something?

472. If a spinner has 4 blue sections, 3 red sections, and 2 yellow sections, which color would you predict that the arrow is most likely to land when you spin it?

473. If you flipped a quarter 8 times, how many times would you predict that the quarter will land on **"heads?"**

474. When we want to find the average of different numbers, what do we need to do after we add them together?

475. What is the average of the numbers 2, 4, and 6?

476. If you scored a 10 on your spelling test, your friend Emily scored a 7, and your friend Avery also scored a 7, what is the average score? $(10+7+7 \div 3 = \_)$

477. If you have a set of numbers from smallest to largest, is the number located in the middle called: the mean, the mode, the median, or the range?

478. What is the mean or average value of the following numbers: 2, 3, 5, and 6? $(2+3+5+6 \div 4 = \_)$

479. If you have a set of numbers what is the number called that is listed most frequently: the mean, the mode, the median, or the range?

480. What is the mode in the following set of numbers: 1, 3, 3, 4, 5, 3, 6, 3?

481. If you have a set of numbers and you want to find the average of those numbers, what would you be finding: the mean, the mode, the median or the range?

482. What is the mean in the following set of numbers: 1, 3, 4, 4? $(1+3+4+4 \div 4 = \_)$

483. What are you finding if you have a set of numbers written in random order and you subtract the smallest value that is listed from the largest value listed: the mean, the mode, the median, or the range?

484. What is the range of the following set of numbers: 0, 1, 5, 4, and 3?

CHAPTER 6

ANSWERS

Language Arts – 4th Grade

1. Language arts
2. Yes, can read silently
3. Yes, can read aloud
4. Yes, can summarize
5. Names short story
6. Names chapter book
7. Names poem
8. No
9. Stanza
10. Refrain
11. Prose
12. Sonnet
13. Fourteen
14. William Shakespeare
15. Names play
16. Yes
17. At the beginning
18. At the end
19. Find page number of topic
20. A glossary
21. The preface
22. The appendix
23. Yes
24. Syllables; part of speech, etc.
25. Hello, et al
26. Yes, can predict
27. Can sequence story events
28. Can identify main idea in text
29. Can state author's purpose
30. Can state supporting details
31. Can compare two stories
32. Both have wicked stepmothers, etc.
33. Can contrast stories
34. Sleeping Beauty was a royal and put under a curse; Cinderella was a commoner who lived with a stepfamily and went to a Ball, etc.
35. Cause and effect
36. Pluto is the farthest planet is cause,
    Pluto is the coldest planet is the effect.
37. Fiction
38. Nonfiction
39. Fable
40. Aesop
41. Tall tale
42. Drama
43. Biography
44. A legend
45. Yes
46. English legend
47. An English legend
48. A myth
49. A Greek myth
50. A ballad
51. A limerick
52. Satire
53. An allegory
54. Epic
55. Literary elements
56. Foreshadowing
57. Hyperbole
58. Simile
59. Metaphor
60. Metaphor
61. Alliteration
62. Onomatopoeia
63. Personification
64. Deep
65. Fall
66. Shop (cabinet)
67. Hatchet
68. Meet
69. Basket
70. Hatch

71. Words
72. Right
73. Him or her
74. Believing
75. None
76. Waste
77. Place
78. Moon
79. Cure
80. Pours
81. Live
82. Thin
83. Drink
84. Etcetera
85. RSVP
86. Can print
87. Can write
88. Can write letter
89. Can write email
90. Can write poem
91. Can write report
92. Bibliography
93. Author, title, publisher, date, etc.
94. Last name
95. Can write book report
96. Can write description
97. Can write a thank you note
98. Can outline main points
99. Can write a summary
100. Can write a summary
101. Writing
102. Rough draft
103. Topic sentence
104. Concluding sentence
105. Can write concluding paragraph
106. Prose
107. Understands transitional words
108. Includes adjectives and verbs
109. Can persuade, inform, entertain
110. Cites persuasive essay
111. Cites informative essay
112. Cites entertaining essay
113. Can write reflective response

114. Internet, Encyclopedia, etc.
115. Encyclopedia
116. Thesaurus
117. Dictionary
118. Atlas
119. Online encyclopedia
120. Has computer skills
121. Familiar with parts of speech
122. Apposition
123. Eight
124. Verb
125. Noun
126. Cheetah
127. Adjective
128. Smart
129. Pronoun
130. He
131. He
132. She
133. It
134. They
135. Personal pronouns
136. Possessive pronouns
137. Verb
138. Jumped
139. Yes
140. Adverb
141. Quickly
142. Well
143. Preposition
144. Prepositions
145. Beside
146. On
147. Prepositional phrases
148. Conjunction
149. And
150. But
151. Interjection
152. Wow!
153. Yes
154. Yes
155. Jack
156. Loves Ice Cream
157. A fragment
158. A fragment
159. I or we, etc.

160. Run-on sentence
161. I went to Chicago. It is a big city.
162. Lisa and Michael made cookies.
163. Am
164. Is
165. Are
166. Lives
167. Was
168. A declarative
169. An interrogative
170. Exclamatory
171. Imperative
172. A declarative
173. Period
174. Interrogative
175. Question mark
176. Pose the words as a question
177. Say the words as a statement
178. An exclamatory sentence
179. Exclamation point
180. Imperative
181. Imperative
182. Comma
183. After the number 7
184. After yes
185. After Orlando
186. Before
187. Before
188. After bones
189. Commas
190. After cookies and brownies
191. Comma
192. Semi-colon
193. Colon
194. Colon
195. Comma
196. Colon
197. Colon
198. Apostrophe
199. Before s (friend's)
200. After
201. Girls'
202. Dog's
203. Apostrophe
204. Letters
205. We're
206. The letter a
207. The letter o
208. Don't
209. I'd
210. They're
211. She is
212. I will
213. You are
214. Did not
215. Will not
216. Quotation marks
217. Yes
218. Before I, after tonight
219. Synonym
220. Clean, etc.
221. Friend, etc.
222. Try, etc.
223. Woman, etc.
224. Different, unknown, etc.
225. Glad, content, etc.
226. Antonym
227. Succeed
228. False
229. Expensive
230. Cloudy
231. Solid
232. Shy
233. Dry
234. Far
235. Under
236. Rough
237. Smooth
238. Prefix
239. Not
240. Im
241. Not possible
242. In
243. Not visible
244. Non
245. Not fiction
246. Wrong
247. Mis
248. Wrongly behave
249. Before
250. pre
251. Before the game
252. in
253. en
254. In danger
255. End of a word
256. -ly

257. -ly
258. -ily
259. -y
260. Full of
261. ful
262. Capable of
263. -able
264. -ible
265. Verb into noun
266. -ment (agreement)
267. Achieve
268. Stem word
269. Deny
270. A palindrome
271. An idiom
272. Hard
273. Says word "action"
274. Says word "actually"
275. Says word "alive"
276. Says word "although"
277. Says word "amount"
278. Says word "area"
279. Says word "blood"
280. Says word "cause"
281. Says word "central"
282. Says word "century"
283. Says word "charcoal"
284. Says word "chart"
285. Says word "check"
286. Says word "club"
287. Says word "colony"
288. Says word "company"
289. Says word "condition"
290. Says word "court"
291. Says word "deal"
292. Says word "death"
293. Says word "describe"
294. Says word "design"
295. Says word "disease"
296. Says word "eleven"
297. Says word "equal"
298. Says word "experience"
299. Says word "factor"
300. Says word "favorite"
301. Says word "figure"
302. Says word "hospital"

303. Says word "include"
304. Says word "increase"
305. Says word "known"
306. Says word "least"
307. Says word "length"
308. Says word "loud"
309. Says word "measure"
310. Says word "molecule"
311. Says word "natural"
312. Says word "necessary"
313. Says word "noun"
314. Says word "oxygen"
315. Says word "phrase"
316. Says word "property"
317. Says word "radio"
318. Says word "receive"
319. Says word "replace"
320. Says word "rhythm"
321. Says word "serve"
322. Says word "similar"
323. Says word "southern"
324. Says word "squirrel"
325. Says word "straight"
326. Says word "subtle"
327. Says word "suffix"
328. Says word "surely"
329. Says word "though"
330. Says word "thought"
331. Says word "touch"
332. Says word "twice"
333. Says word "used"
334. Says word "usually"
335. Says word "view"
336. Says word "weight"
337. Says word "wheat"
338. Says word "whom"
339. Says word "young"

ANSWERS –
Social Studies – 4th Grade

1. Earth
2. Globe
3. Seven
4. Pacific and Atlantic
5. Asia, North America, South America, Africa, Australia, Europe, and Australia/Oceania
6. Can read map
7. Types of maps
8. The equator
9. The prime meridian
10. Hemisphere
11. Four
12. Northern Hemisphere
13. Southern Hemisphere
14. Eastern Hemisphere
15. Western Hemisphere
16. The prime meridian
17. Eastern and Western
18. Parallels
19. Meridians
20. Longitude
21. Latitude
22. East to West
23. North to South
24. The prime meridian
25. Greenwich
26. Yes
27. Degree
28. 0
29. 180
30. The International Dateline
31. A coordinate
32. 30 degrees north of equator 20 degrees east
33. Can find coordinates
34. Can identify states on map
35. Can identify city on map
36. Can follow building map
37. Scale
38. Yes, maps have scales
39. A state map
40. A city map
41. A country map
42. A political map
43. A physical map
44. A historical map
45. A relief map
46. A resource map
47. A product map
48. A road map
49. A climate map
50. A topographic map
51. A topographic map
52. The Rockies
53. Mount McKinley
54. The Appalachian Mountains
55. The Rockies
56. The Appalachians
57. Erosion
58. Mountain state
59. The Andes Mountains
60. Mount Aconcagua
61. The Incas
62. Machu Picchu
63. The Atlas Mountains
64. The Eastern Highlands
65. Mount Kilimanjaro
66. The Alps
67. The Alps
68. Mont Blanc
69. The Ural Mountains
70. Mount Fuji
71. The Himalayas
72. Mount Everest
73. Mount Everest
74. Less oxygen
75. The Rockies and Appalachians
76. Yes, can be divided
77. Mid-Atlantic
78. The Midwest
79. The Pacific Northwest
80. Rocky Mountain
81. New England
82. South Atlantic States
83. The Southwest
84. Canada
85. Mexico
86. Alaska and Hawaii
87. A relief map

88. Channel
89. A Strait
90. A delta
91. A prairie
92. A plateau
93. A mesa
94. A cliff
95. A canyon
96. The Grand Canyon
97. A basin
98. A cape
99. Cape Cod
100. A gulf
101. The Gulf of Mexico
102. The Persian Gulf
103. A bay
104. A desert
105. The Sahara
106. Antarctica
107. The Mojave
108. The Atacama
109. The Arabian
110. A peninsula
111. An isthmus
112. A fjord
113. A lake
114. A river
115. Names famous lakes
116. Huron, Ontario, Michigan, Eric, and Superior
117. Great Salt Lake
118. Amazon, Nile, Mississippi, etc.
119. Missouri, Mississippi, etc.
120. Rio Grande
121. The Amazon
122. The Nile
123. The Yellow
124. The Yangtze
125. The Ganges
126. The Volga
127. The Danube
128. The Rhine
129. The Seine
130. The Thames
131. The Mississippi
132. A tributary
133. Tributaries
134. Delta
135. North America (or other)
136. Names continents
137. Asia
138. China
139. Antarctica
140. Europe
141. Scandinavia
142. The British Isles
143. Africa
144. Asia
145. South America
146. Provinces
147. North America
148. French and English
149. States
150. North America
151. Spanish
152. 48
153. Alaska and Hawaii
154. Hawaii
155. Alaska
156. Arizona
157. New Mexico
158. Oklahoma
159. Utah
160. Wyoming
161. Idaho
162. Washington
163. Montana
164. South Dakota
165. North Dakota
166. Colorado
167. Nebraska
168. Nevada
169. West Virginia
170. Kansas
171. Oregon
172. Minnesota
173. California
174. Wisconsin
175. Iowa
176. Texas
177. Florida
178. Michigan

179. Arkansas
180. Missouri
181. Maine
182. Alabama
183. Illinois
184. Mississippi
185. Indiana
186. Louisiana
187. Ohio
188. Tennessee
189. Kentucky
190. Vermont
191. Rhode Island
192. North Carolina
193. New York
194. Virginia
195. New Hampshire
196. South Carolina
197. Maryland
198. Massachusetts
199. Connecticut
200. Georgia
201. New Jersey
202. Pennsylvania
203. Delaware
204. Texas
205. Rhode Island
206. Washington D.C.
207. District of Columbia
208. The Atlantic
209. The Pacific
210. Canada
211. Mexico
212. Names bordering states
213. Names bordering counties
214. Yes
215. The American Flag
216. 13
217. The Pledge of Allegiance
218. Betsy Ross
219. The Liberty Bell
220. The Bald Eagle
221. The Statue of Liberty
222. The Declaration of Independence
223. The United States Constitution
224. The Star-Spangled Banner
225. Flags, birds, songs, etc.

226. Mount Rushmore
227. Roosevelt
228. Washington D.C.
229. The White House
230. Virginia
231. The Washington Monument
232. Iwo Jima
233. Niagara Falls
234. National Parks
235. Names states' monuments
236. Yes
237. Ancient history
238. Prehistory
239. Mesopotamia
240. Iraq
241. Mesopotamia
242. The Tigris and Euphrates
243. A class system
244. Babylon
245. Hammurabi
246. Mesopotamia
247. Yes
248. Cuneiform
249. Mesopotamia
250. Sumerians
251. The Assyrians
252. The Sumerians
253. The seed plow
254. 60
255. Ziggurats
256. The Hanging Gardens
257. The Middle Ages
258. Medieval
259. The peasants
260. Serf
261. The Barbarians
262. Byzantine
263. Constantinople
264. The Huns
265. Attila
266. Stirrups
267. The Vandals
268. The Visigoths
269. The Angles
270. The Saxons
271. Dark Ages
272. Christianity
273. The Pope
274. Judaism

275. Monks
276. Nuns
277. Charlemagne
278. Feudalism
279. Nobility, church, and commoners
280. The king
281. The vassal
282. The lord
283. A fief
284. Yes
285. Knights
286. A serf
287. A castle
288. A minstrel
289. A jester
290. Croquet
291. A page
292. A squire
293. The Canterbury Tales
294. A knight
295. To sew, weave, and spin
296. Jousting
297. Chivalry
298. Yes
299. Yes, merchants held power
300. A guild
301. An apprentice
302. A journeyman
303. A master
304. Yes, religion important
305. Yes, became stronger
306. A strong kingdom
307. England
308. William the Conqueror
309. Yes, Anglo-Saxons objected
310. William II
311. Yes, inherited throne
312. Yes, established strong government
313. Yes, established common law
314. Gave up land to France
315. Counts, dukes, lords, and earls
316. The Magna Carta
317. A Parliament
318. Black Death

319. The Hundred Years' War
320. Joan of Arc
321. Yes, considered the same
322. The Byzantine Empire
323. World religions
324. Islam
325. Mecca
326. Kaaba
327. Dome of the Rock
328. Medina
329. Hijra
330. A Mosque
331. The Grand Mosque
332. The Prophet's Mosque
333. Jihad
334. The Quran
335. The Five Pillars of Islam
336. Yes, Muslims conquered other places
337. Yes, Muslims lived in Spain
338. The Alhambra
339. Córdoba
340. Yes, it is a holy city
341. The Crusades
342. Arabic numerals
343. The Moors
344. Africa
345. Sahara
346. Atlas
347. Savanna
348. The Congo
349. Africa
350. Egypt
351. Pharaoh
352. Yes, Pharaoh as God
353. Yes, had hierarchy of rulers
354. Second in power
355. The Vizier
356. Yes, citizens paid taxes
357. Dynasty
358. Yes, Egypt ruled by dynasties
359. Upper and Lower Egypt
360. King Menes
361. Memphis
362. Thebes
363. Cairo

364. Giza
365. Pyramid of Khufu
366. The Great Pyramid of Giza
367. The Great Sphinx
368. To guard the temples and tombs
369. 240 feet long
370. The nose
371. Erosion
372. Pillar
373. Nefertiti
374. King Tutankhamen
375. Ramses II
376. The cobra goddess
377. The Valley of the Kings
378. Howard Carter
379. Paintings
380. The Book of the Dead
381. Vandals
382. Mummification
383. Yes
384. Decimal system
385. Hieroglyphics
386. Consonant sounds
387. Scribes
388. Scribes
389. The Rosetta Stone
390. Farmers
391. Yes
392. Necklaces
393. Mud bricks
394. Bread
395. The Egyptians
396. The Persians
397. The Kingdom of Kush
398. Alexander the Great
399. Ptolemaic
400. Cleopatra
401. The Valley of the Kings
402. The Nile
403. A tributary
404. Yes, has many landforms
405. Papyrus
406. Papyrus
407. Papyrus reeds
408. Reed boats
409. The camel
410. A caravan
411. Papyrus
412. No, did not have army
413. A chariot
414. West African Empires
415. Mansa Musa
416. Griots
417. 54 nations
418. Africa
419. Malaria
420. One billion
421. Charles Darwin
422. Sudan
423. Mt. Kilimanjaro
424. Cape of Good Hope
425. The Suez Canal
426. The Aswan Dam
427. Anwar Sadat
428. Ivory Coast
429. The Nile and the Congo
430. The Sahara and Kalahari
431. Yes, could fit into U.S. borders
432. The Savanna
433. Elephants, zebras, giraffes, etc.
434. Elephants
435. Elephants, giraffes, lions, etc.
436. Kenya
437. The cheetah
438. African languages
439. 2000 languages
440. Yes, tribes speak unique language
441. Arabic
442. Islam
443. Ramadan
444. Madagascar
445. Masks
446. Drums
447. Nelson Mandela
448. Apartheid
449. Muammar Gaddafi
450. Yes, celebrate both holidays
451. Kwanzaa
452. "The Lion King"
453. Asia
454. 48
455. Vatican City
456. Russia
457. China
458. Dynasties

---

459. Qin Shi Huang
460. Yes, Huang made improvements
461. The Great Wall of China
462. Terracotta
463. Han Dynasty
464. Yes, changed his name
465. Yes, credited with inventions
466. Confucius
467. Civil service
468. Yes, had respect philosophy
469. Schools
470. Silk
471. Yes, wanted to keep it secret
472. Birds and flowers
473. Clothing
474. Upper class
475. The Silk Road
476. Trade and commerce
477. Yes, Silk Road important
478. Buddhism
479. Tang
480. Trading
481. A camel
482. Woodblock printing
483. A book
484. Gunpowder
485. Porcelain
486. Poetry
487. Confucianism
488. Tea
489. Toilet paper
490. Paper
491. The Great Wall
492. After the Tang Dynasty
493. Magnetic compass and iron plow
494. Books
495. Yes, one of most advanced civilizations
496. Rice
497. Tall pagodas
498. Mongolia
499. Gobi
500. The Chinese
501. The abacus
502. Beijing
503. Merchant associations
504. Marco Polo
505. The Silk Road
506. Ming
507. Porcelain pottery
508. White
509. Blue
510. China
511. Silk Scrolls
512. Calligraphy
513. The Three Perfections
514. Lacquer
515. Landscapes
516. The Great Wall
517. The longest man-made structure
518. The wheelbarrow
519. Grand Canal
520. The Forbidden City
521. Imperial Palace
522. 24
523. Before Columbus
524. India and Africa
525. Religions
526. Nepal
527. Yin and Yang
528. Feng Shui
529. The Yellow and Yangtze
530. The dragon
531. Imperial power
532. The New Year
533. Chopsticks
534. Bamboo
535. The Giant Panda
536. China
537. Two
538. An animal
539. The Himalayas
540. Mt. Everest
541. K2
542. China
543. The People's Republic of China
544. Hong Kong
545. Communist country

546. Beijing
547. Tiananmen Square
548. Shanghai
549. Mandarin
550. Seven
551. Yes, many speak English
552. Symbols
553. Chinese
554. Shoes
555. Lion Dance and Dragon Dance
556. Kung Fu
557. Zodiac
558. Christopher Columbus
559. The Age of Discovery
560. The 1600's
561. Great Britain
562. The French and Indian War
563. The Seven Years War
564. Taxes
565. "Taxation without representation"
566. The Stamp Act
567. Protest and boycott British products
568. The Colonial Congress
569. The Sons of Liberty
570. The Townshend Acts
571. Protested and rebelled
572. The Boston Massacre
573. The Boston Tea Party
574. The Intolerable Acts
575. The First Continental Congress
576. Patrick Henry
577. Thomas Paine
578. Thomas Paine
579. Patriots
580. Founding Fathers
581. Loyalists
582. Lexington and Concord
583. Yes, keeping eye on British
584. Paul Revere
585. William Dawes
586. Lanterns
587. Redcoats
588. "The Redcoats are coming."
589. Lexington and Concord
590. Yes, managed to escape
591. Minutemen
592. Yes, had both

593. Muskets
594. Lexington
595. Still uncertain
596. The Americans
597. Boston
598. Lt. Colonel Francis Smith
599. Captain John Parker
600. Bunker and Breeds
601. Took place on Breeds Hill
602. British
603. The whites of their eyes
604. The British
605. Land and freedom
606. The Second Continental Congress
607. George Washington
608. The eagle
609. 5,000 African Americans fought
610. Thomas Jefferson
611. July 4, 1776
612. July 4th
613. 56
614. John Hancock
615. Yes, copies sent to all 13 colonies
616. Yes, all states declared free
617. The National Archives
618. Yes, war still going on
619. Money and land
620. Delaware
621. An American flag
622. June 14th
623. Yes, flag had many transformations
624. 50 stars
625. The American flag
626. Saratoga
627. France
628. France
629. Yes, women helped war effort
630. Benedict Arnold
631. Valley Forge
632. Yorktown
633. The Treaty of Paris
634. The American Revolution
635. Yes, adopted own constitution
636. The Articles of Confederation
637. Shays' Rebellion

638. The Virginia Plan
639. The Federalist Papers
640. The Bill of Rights
641. The Constitutional Convention
642. Executive
643. Judicial
644. Legislative
645. The Connecticut Compromise
646. The House and the Senate
647. Two
648. 100
649. Number based on population
650. 435
651. The Three-Fifths Compromise
652. 20
653. The U.S. Constitution
654. The Preamble
655. Checks and balances
656. Yes, has veto power
657. 1790
658. An amendment
659. The Bill of Rights
660. The First Amendment
661. Yes
662. The President
663. The governor
664. Names state governor
665. The mayor
666. Names city mayor
667. Taxes
668. Yes
669. President Lincoln
670. George Washington
671. Martha Washington
672. John Adams
673. Cabinet
674. Yes
675. Secretary
676. 15
677. Secretary of State
678. Yes
679. Yes, AG part of cabinet
680. Thomas Jefferson
681. Alexander Hamilton
682. Four
683. Two

684. Yes
685. Democratic-Republican
686. Federalist
687. Democratic-Republican and Federalist
688. Republican and Democrat
689. New York City
690. Washington D.C.
691. The White House
692. Mount Vernon
693. The U.S. Capitol
694. John Adams
695. Jefferson
696. Abigail Adams
697. Thomas Jefferson
698. France
699. Louisiana
700. Napoleon Bonaparte
701. The Louisiana Purchase
702. Lewis and Clark
703. Two years
704. Kept detailed journals
705. James Madison
706. The War of 1812
707. USS Constitution
708. The Capitol
709. The Treaty of Ghent
710. The Battle of New Orleans
711. James Monroe
712. Yes
713. The South
714. The North
715. Abolitionists
716. The Missouri Compromise
717. The Monroe Doctrine
718. John Quincy Adams
719. Andrew Jackson
720. Transfer Indian land
721. The Indian Removal Act
722. The Trail of Tears
723. Reformer
724. Dorothea Dix
725. Horace Mann
726. Lucretia Mott and Elizabeth Stanton
727. Amelia Bloomer

728. Sojourner Truth

ANSWERS –
Civics – 4th Grade

1. Laws
2. Yes
3. Executive, legislative, and judicial
4. Federal
5. Federal
6. State
7. Local
8. The Declaration of Independence
9. Founding Fathers
10. The Preamble
11. An ordinance
12. The U.S. Constitution
13. An amendment
14. The Bill of Rights
15. The legislative branch
16. The House and the Senate
17. The U.S. Capitol
18. Names state capital
19. A legislator
20. The executive branch
21. The judicial branch
22. Checks and Balances
23. Separation of Powers
24. The President
25. Names current President
26. Names current Vice-President
27. The White House
28. The President
29. Pennsylvania Avenue
30. Veto power
31. Supreme
32. A judge
33. A jury
34. Senate and the House
35. 435
36. Yes
37. 100
38. Two per state
39. The Speaker
40. Two years
41. Two
42. Six years
43. A bill
44. A law
45. Veto
46. A mayor
47. Names city mayor
48. A governor
49. Names state governor
50. Local

ANSWERS:
Science – 4th Grade

1. Yes
2. Physical
3. Equal to
4. Yes
5. Solids, liquids, and gases
6. Plasmas
7. Yes
8. Man-made plasma
9. Solid
10. Liquid
11. Gas
12. Helium
13. Yes
14. Solid to liquid
15. Liquid to gas
16. Evaporation
17. Steam
18. Evaporation
19. Condensation
20. Frost
21. Rust
22. Visible
23. Invisible
24. Beach ball, etc.
25. Basketball, stone, etc.
26. Yes
27. 118
28. An atom
29. Molecules
30. An element
31. Yes
32. Periodic Table
33. A compound
34. Water
35. True
36. A property
37. Yes
38. Physical properties
39. Physical
40. Periodic
41. Nonmetals
42. Penny, pipes, etc.
43. Trumpet, bed, etc.
44. Appliances, cookware, etc.
45. Bells, statues, Olympic medals, etc.
46. Buckles, keys, earrings, etc.
47. Jewelry, coins, Olympic medals…
48. Silverware, jewelry, coins, etc.
49. Nails, cans, pots, etc.
50. Cans, foil, tinsel, etc.
51. Cans, baseball bats, siding, etc.
52. Volume
53. Capacity
54. Grams
55. Liters
56. A balance
57. Energy
58. Potential and Kinetic
59. Potential
60. Kinetic
61. Yes
62. Forms of energy
63. Potential to kinetic
64. Energy
65. Pushing a wheelbarrow
66. Solar
67. Mechanical
68. Yes
69. Chemical
70. Coal
71. Electrical
72. Potential
73. Kinetic
74. Potential
75. Kinetic
76. Potential to Kinetic
77. Electrical
78. Mechanical
79. Heat
80. Chemical
81. Gravitational
82. Chemical
83. Yes
84. Renewable
85. Non-renewable
86. Force
87. Yes
88. Motion
89. Yes

90.	Yes	136.	Copper
91.	Speed	137.	Iron
92.	A force	138.	Electromagnetic lines
93.	Gravity	139.	Low voltage
94.	A force	140.	Current
95.	Both	141.	Direct Current
96.	Balanced forces	142.	AC
97.	Balanced	143.	Amperes or amps
98.	Balanced	144.	Static
99.	Friction	145.	Yes
100.	Slows it down	146.	An electromagnet
101.	Yes	147.	Yes
102.	Heat	148.	Electromagnets
103.	Inertia	149.	Electric
104.	The first law of motion	150.	Yes
105.	Sir Isaac Newton	151.	Michael Faraday
106.	Apple fell out of tree	152.	Thomas Edison
107.	Opposite reaction	153.	Benjamin Franklin
108.	Inertia	154.	Thomas Edison
109.	More inertia	155.	Light
110.	Simple machines	156.	Sunlight
111.	Simple machines	157.	Visible
112.	A wedge	158.	Yes
113.	A lever	159.	Red, orange, yellow, green, blue, indigo, and violet
114.	A wheel and axle		
115.	An inclined plane	160.	Red
116.	A pulley	161.	Violet
117.	A screw	162.	Yes
118.	Compound	163.	Reflects
119.	Complex	164.	Yes
120.	Complex	165.	In waves
121.	Lever, wheel and axle	166.	White light
122.	Appliances, lamps, etc.	167.	Black light
123.	A circuit	168.	A crest and a trough
124.	Positive	169.	Yes
125.	Open	170.	A wavelength
126.	Conductors	171.	A trough
127.	Conductors	172.	A crest
128.	Insulators	173.	Radar
129.	Series	174.	8 minutes
130.	Parallel	175.	Light
131.	Closed	176.	Light travels faster
132.	Open	177.	A vacuum
133.	A closed circuit	178.	Light
134.	A series circuit	179.	Yes
135.	A parallel circuit	180.	Light

181.	Laser	229.	Decibels
182.	Insects	230.	An echo
183.	Smooth	231.	Mach 1
184.	Light	232.	Our ears
185.	Refracted	233.	Life Science
186.	Refracted	234.	Cells
187.	Yes	235.	Kingdoms
188.	Transmitted	236.	Kingdoms
189.	Light that passes through object	237.	Plants
		238.	Says name of plant
190.	Transparent	239.	Vascular and nonvascular
191.	Translucent	240.	Yes
192.	Opaque	241.	Spore-producing
193.	Absorbed	242.	Seed-producing
194.	Reflect	243.	Seeds
195.	Dark clothing	244.	Flowering
196.	Translucent	245.	The sepals
197.	Transparent	246.	Photosynthesis
198.	Opaque	247.	Pollination
199.	Lens	248.	Plant reproduction
200.	Lenses	249.	Producers
201.	Refraction	250.	The root
202.	Convex and concave	251.	The leaves
203.	Convergent and divergent	252.	The stem
204.	Convex	253.	The pistil
205.	Concave	254.	The stamen
206.	Convex	255.	Pollination
207.	Concave	256.	Spores
208.	Convex	257.	Photosynthesis
209.	Microscope	258.	Food
210.	Telescope	259.	Sunlight
211.	Binoculars	260.	Chlorophyll
212.	Sound	261.	Dormancy
213.	In waves	262.	The soil
214.	Yes	263.	The constants
215.	The frequency of sound	264.	Consumers
216.	Hertz	265.	Producers
217.	The wavelength of sound	266.	Decomposers
218.	Pitch	267.	A decomposer
219.	Fast	268.	Sun, producer, consumer, decomposer
220.	Slow		
221.	Low pitch	269.	An ecosystem
222.	High pitch	270.	A biome
223.	Quicker	271.	Waste, cut down trees, etc.
224.	Gases	272.	Food chain
225.	Steel	273.	The Sun
226.	Yes	274.	Niche
227.	Vibrate	275.	Habitat
228.	Volume	276.	Adaptation

277.	Behavioral	322.	A fault
278.	Structural	323.	Tectonic plates
279.	Earth Science	324.	The San Andreas Fault
280.	The Solar System	325.	An earthquake
281.	The Sun	326.	Seismic waves
282.	Eight	327.	The epicenter
283.	A dwarf planet	328.	The epicenter
284.	Another dwarf planet	329.	Seismologists
285.	Inner planets	330.	A seismograph
286.	Outer planets	331.	Magnitude
287.	Third planet from the Sun	332.	Richter scale
288.	4.5 billion years old	333.	A tsunami
289.	150 kilometers	334.	Yes
290.	93 million	335.	An avalanche
291.	The ozone layer	336.	A landslide
292.	Atmosphere, water, and energy	337.	A mudslide
		338.	An avalanche
293.	The Earth	339.	A volcano
294.	The Sun	340.	Lava
295.	The Sun	341.	Along the edges
296.	4.5 billion years	342.	Mountains
297.	One	343.	Active
298.	24 hours	344.	Dormant
299.	Day and night	345.	Mount Vesuvius
300.	Summer	346.	Mount Saint Helens
301.	Winter	347.	A hot spring
302.	Spring	348.	A geyser
303.	The moon	349.	Old Faithful
304.	Mars	350.	Pangaea
305.	The moon	351.	Continental drift
306.	Moon phases	352.	3
307.	Tides	353.	Dome
308.	Lunar	354.	Folded
309.	Solar	355.	Folded
310.	Four	356.	Fault-block mountains
311.	Lithosphere	357.	Rocks
312.	The inner core	358.	Minerals
313.	The crust	359.	How they were formed
314.	The mantle	360.	3
315.	The outer core	361.	Yes
316.	The inner core	362.	Igneous
317.	Plates	363.	Yes
318.	Plate Tectonics	364.	Sedimentary
319.	Convergent	365.	Metamorphic
320.	Divergent	366.	Yes
321.	Continental drift	367.	Physical weathering

368.	Chemical weathering	417.	Low pressure
369.	Erosion	418.	A front
370.	Topsoil	419.	A warm front
371.	Subsoil	420.	A cold front
372.	Bedrock	421.	A warm front
373.	Yes	422.	A cold front
374.	Glaciers	423.	Yes
375.	The Ice Age	424.	Cirrus
376.	Great Lakes	425.	Cumulus
377.	Great Lakes	426.	Stratus
378.	Glaciers	427.	Cumulonimbus
379.	Montana	428.	Thunderheads
380.	Alaska	429.	Lightning
381.	Describes today's weather	430.	Thunder
382.	Meteorology	431.	186,000 miles per second
383.	The atmosphere	432.	A barometer
384.	The atmosphere	433.	A hygrometer
385.	4	434.	A rain gauge
386.	Yes	435.	Wind
387.	Exosphere	436.	Wind
388.	Troposphere	437.	A breeze
389.	The ozone layer	438.	A gale
390.	Mesosphere	439.	A hurricane
391.	Precipitation	440.	Yes
392.	Water cycle	441.	Tornado
393.	Rain	442.	A hurricane
394.	Dew	443.	The eye
395.	Fog	444.	An anemometer
396.	Hail	445.	Prevailing winds
397.	Snow	446.	Trade winds
398.	Frost	447.	Coriolis Effect
399.	Temperature	448.	A jet stream
400.	Thermometer	449.	Tidal waves
401.	Celsius	450.	A sandstorm
402.	Degrees Fahrenheit	451.	A blizzard
403.	Visibility	452.	Climate
404.	Yes	453.	Climates
405.	A flood	454.	Tropical
406.	A drought	455.	Polar
407.	Temperature	456.	Habitat
408.	Humidity	457.	Yes
409.	Weight of the air	458.	Season
410.	Cold air	459.	Yes
411.	Hot air	460.	Equator
412.	A cold air mass	461.	Opposite
413.	Warm	462.	The same
414.	Air masses	463.	June 21st
415.	Air pocket	464.	Winter
416.	High pressure	465.	September 21st

466.	December 21st	512.	The four blood types
467.	March 21st	513.	The Rh factor
468.	Autumn	514.	Type O
469.	Yes	515.	Positive
470.	Monsoon	516.	Compatible blood type
471.	Typhoon	517.	Blood clots
472.	States weather preference	518.	Yes
473.	States climate preference	519.	States blood type
474.	Anatomy	520.	Different
475.	Names outside body parts	521.	Yes
476.	Names inside body parts	522.	Circulatory
477.	A muscle	523.	Respiratory
478.	Your skin	524.	20,000
479.	The heart	525.	Respiratory
480.	Yes	526.	Lungs
481.	Four	527.	Trachea
482.	Atria	528.	Bronchial tubes
483.	Ventricles	529.	Alveoli
484.	4	530.	The diaphragm
485.	Valves	531.	Smoking
486.	The aorta	532.	Eat well, exercise, etc.
487.	Blood vessels		
488.	Arteries		
489.	Veins		
490.	Capillaries		
491.	Blood pressure		
492.	Pulse		
493.	60		
494.	Goes up		
495.	Blood		
496.	Carbon dioxide		
497.	Plasma		
498.	Red and white		
499.	Hemoglobin		
500.	White		
501.	Platelets		
502.	Four months		
503.	8 million per second		
504.	Liver		
505.	Spleen		
506.	Heart		
507.	Heart attack (Cardiac arrest)		
508.	Saturated fats		
509.	Cardiac arrest		
510.	A transfusion		
511.	Four		

ANSWERS –
Math – 4th Grade

1. Ten
2. 1
3. Hundred
4. 2
5. One thousand
6. 3
7. Ten thousand
8. 4
9. One hundred thousand
10. 5
11. One million
12. 6
13. Ten million
14. One hundred million
15. One billion
16. One trillion
17. Stars, National Debt, etc.
18. A comma
19. 3
20. One million, four hundred thirty-four thousand, five hundred and sixty-seven.
21. No
22. Yes
23. 3
24. 5
25. 6
26. 4
27. Ten
28. A decade
29. A century
30. 100,500
31. Eight thousand, two hundred and forty-three
32. 5,040
33. Positive
34. Negative
35. Even
36. Odd
37. Yes
38. Yes
39. Arabic
40. I, II, III, IV, and V

41. VI, VII, VIII, IX, and X
42. 50
43. 100
44. 500
45. 1,000
46. Subtract
47. 40
48. Add
49. 60
50. 1,150
51. 18
52. MMXXI
53. Yes
54. Down
55. Up
56. 3,000
57. 2,000
58. 2,900
59. 2,260
60. A prime number
61. A composite number
62. A prime number
63. No
64. Prime numbers
65. Composite numbers
66. Composite number
67. Prime number
68. Yes
69. 140,000
70. One million
71. 6,352
72. The associative
73. The commutative
74. The identity
75. 8,000
76. Yes
77. Yes
78. 101,000
79. 165,000
80. 350,000
81. 500
82. Yes
83. 3 and 8
84. 24
85. 4, 6, 8, 10, etc.
86. 12, 18, 24, 30, etc.
87. 7
88. 9
89. 6 and 9

90.	12	135.	The divisor
91.	A square	136.	20
92.	Yes	137.	Yes, remembers division facts to 12
93.	4	138.	That number
94.	25	139.	1
95.	36	140.	12/3
96.	49	141.	4
97.	56	142.	A factor
98.	81	143.	1,2, and 4
99.	100	144.	1,2,3,4,6,8,12, and 24
100.	2	145.	1,2, and 4
101.	6	146.	2 Remainder 1
102.	5	147.	4 Remainder 2
103.	9	148.	132
104.	7	149.	81
105.	11	150.	321
106.	8	151.	8 x 3 = 24
107.	12	152.	90
108.	24	153.	60
109.	0	154.	8 Remainder 3
110.	440	155.	Less than
111.	2200	156.	Greater than
112.	Yes	157.	Greater than
113.	Add them	158.	Yes
114.	4	159.	Algebra
115.	80,000	160.	20
116.	The identity	161.	7
117.	The distributive	162.	6
118.	The associative	163.	Yes
119.	The zero property of multiplication	164.	Yes
120.	Identity property	165.	24
121.	Yes	166.	4
122.	12,000	167.	15
123.	Greater than	168.	Dollar
124.	Equal to	169.	Euro, Pound, Yen, etc.
125.	Less than	170.	Letter "S" with two lines through it
126.	Division	171.	Letter "C" with line through it
127.	20 ÷ 2 = 10	172.	$1.25
128.	3 x 8 = 24	173.	A fifty-dollar bill
129.	20	174.	$490
130.	5	175.	$500
131.	4	176.	$30
132.	9	177.	Yes (No)
133.	The dividend		
134.	The quotient		

178.	85 cents
179.	$45
180.	$7
181.	$5.50
182.	48
183.	$4.80
184.	$4.00
185.	George Washington
186.	Abraham Lincoln
187.	Alexander Hamilton
188.	Andrew Jackson
189.	Ulysses S. Grant
190.	Abraham Lincoln
191.	Thomas Jefferson
192.	Franklin D. Roosevelt
193.	George Washington
194.	Seconds, minutes, hours, days, weeks, months, year
195.	365 ¼
196.	Add one day, February 29th, every four years
197.	182 ½
198.	24 hours
199.	12 hours
200.	6 hours
201.	18 hours
202.	60 seconds
203.	60 minutes
204.	1 ½ hours
205.	30 minutes
206.	15 minutes
207.	75 minutes
208.	192 minutes
209.	2 minutes, four seconds
210.	135 minutes
211.	21 days
212.	Time zones
213.	Names time zone
214.	Yes
215.	9:25
216.	Twenty minutes to ten
217.	2:25
218.	6:30
219.	Yes, can read a schedule
220.	U.S. customary units
221.	Inches, feet, yards, miles
222.	12
223.	½, ¼, 1/16, 1/8, etc.
224.	Estimate
225.	3 feet
226.	4 feet
227.	36
228.	18
229.	A mile
230.	2,640
231.	A mile
232.	6 feet
233.	Ounces, pounds, tons
234.	16
235.	8
236.	12
237.	32
238.	Pounds
239.	3 pounds
240.	Oz.
241.	Lb.
242.	2000 pounds
243.	3 tons
244.	T
245.	7 pounds
246.	Cup, pint, quart, gallon
247.	Teaspoon, tablespoon, cup, stick (of butter)
248.	3
249.	Tsp.
250.	Tbsp.
251.	8 fluid ounces
252.	C.
253.	½, 1/3, ¼, 1 cup
254.	8
255.	2
256.	Pt.
257.	2
258.	Qt.
259.	4
260.	3 pints
261.	3 and 1/3
262.	Metric
263.	Decimal
264.	10
265.	100
266.	1000
267.	10
268.	3.2
269.	Cm.
270.	Mm.
271.	100
272.	M.

273.	A meter	318.	Yes
274.	1000	319.	¼
275.	Km.	320.	2/3
276.	A kilometer	321.	Mixed
277.	62	322.	2 and 2/5
278.	Liter	323.	Multiply 4x6 plus 1 over 4
279.	100	324.	14/3
280.	1000	325.	6
281.	Cl.	326.	6
282.	L.	327.	4
283.	500	328.	Adding the numerators
284.	Milligram, gram, kilogram, metric ton	329.	4/5
		330.	12/9
285.	1000	331.	10/10 or 1
286.	10	332.	1 and 1/3
287.	Mg.	333.	4/7
288.	Cg.	334.	Find LCM first
289.	1000	335.	5/6
290.	G.	336.	Find LCM first
291.	100	337.	1/3
292.	Kg.	338.	4/9
293.	Metric system	339.	1 and ½ pounds left
294.	Celsius	340.	2 and 2/3
295.	Fahrenheit	341.	2 feet
296.	0	342.	½ foot
297.	Freezes	343.	6 inches
298.	Fractions	344.	Less than
299.	2	345.	Equal to
300.	10	346.	Equal to
301.	½	347.	Yes
302.	¼	348.	¼, 1/3, ½, and 1
303.	Yes	349.	1/8, ¼, ½, and 1
304.	6/8, 9/16, etc.	350.	½
305.	2/6, 3/9, etc.	351.	¼
306.	3/5	352.	1 and ½
307.	4/8	353.	2/9
308.	Improper fraction	354.	2/10 or 1/5
309.	1	355.	¼
310.	Improper	356.	½
311.	Yes	357.	¾
312.	A whole number	358.	With decimals
313.	4	359.	$6.75
314.	1	360.	$1.25
315.	0	361.	10
316.	Division	362.	A decade
317.	Yes, to 2/5	363.	Two point five zero

364.	.1	413.	270 degrees
365.	.01	414.	360 degrees
366.	.001	415.	Intersecting
367.	Equal to	416.	Perpendicular
368.	Yes	417.	Parallel
369.	Greater than	418.	Horizontal
370.	2.4	419.	Vertical
371.	¼	420.	Diagonal
372.	¾	421.	A polygon
373.	½	422.	A triangle
374.	0	423.	A quadrilateral
375.	3.280	424.	A square and a rectangle
376.	4.9	425.	A parallelogram
377.	4.80	426.	A trapezoid
378.	3.300	427.	A square
379.	3.500	428.	A rhombus
380.	3.250	429.	A quadrilateral
381.	6	430.	A pentagon
382.	Yes, can read decimals	431.	A hexagon
383.	1.8	432.	A heptagon
384.	Decimal points	433.	An octagon
385.	A zero	434.	A nonagon
386.	7	435.	A decagon
387.	2.9	436.	Octopus
388.	5	437.	A hexagon
389.	.9 centimeters	438.	A rhombus
390.	Equal to	439.	Congruent
391.	Geometry	440.	Similar
392.	A line	441.	Symmetrical
393.	Letters	442.	Its center
394.	An arrow	443.	Area
395.	A ray	444.	32 centimeters
396.	The end point	445.	9 feet
397.	An angle	446.	Yes
398.	The vertex	447.	144 inches
399.	Three	448.	Square foot, acre, square mile
400.	A right angle	449.	Square centimeter, square meter, hectare, square kilometer
401.	90 degrees		
402.	Acute		
403.	Obtuse		
404.	Yes	450.	2 dimensional
405.	Isosceles	451.	Yes
406.	Equilateral	452.	A prism
407.	Scalene	453.	A cylinder
408.	Right	454.	A pyramid
409.	A protractor	455.	A sphere
410.	50 degrees	456.	A cube
411.	180 degrees	457.	A cone
412.	90 degrees	458.	The surface area

459.	Yes
460.	The volume
461.	12
462.	No
463.	A compass
464.	Radius
465.	Diameter
466.	A chord
467.	The diameter
468.	The radius
469.	16 cm (D=Rx2)
470.	Its circumference
471.	Yes, can predict
472.	Blue
473.	4
474.	Divide by the total numbers
475.	4
476.	8
477.	The median
478.	4
479.	The mode
480.	3
481.	The median
482.	3
483.	The range
484.	5

BIBLIOGRAPHY

"Ducksters: Education Site for Kids and Teachers." *Ducksters: Education Site for Kids and Teachers*. N.p., n.d. Web. Accessed 2018. http://www.ducksters.com.

"ENCHANTED LEARNING HOME PAGE." *ENCHANTED LEARNING HOME PAGE*. N.p., n.d. Web. 10 Accessed 2018. http://www.enchantedlearning.com.

"Fact Monster from Information Please." *Fact Monster: Online Almanac, Dictionary, Encyclopedia, and Homework Help*. N.p., n.d. Web. Accessed 2018. http://www.factmonster.com.

Grade Level Help at Internet 4 Classrooms." *Grade Level Help at Internet 4 Classrooms*. N.p., n.d. Web. Accessed 2019. http://www.internet4classrooms.com .

Hirsch, E. D. *What Your First Grader Needs to Know: Fundamentals of a Good First-Grade Education*. New York: Doubleday, 1991. Print.

Hirsch, E. D. *What Your Third Grader Needs to Know: Fundamentals of a Good Third-Grade Education*. New York: Doubleday, 1992. Print.

Hirsch, E. D. *What Your Fourth Grader Needs to Know: Fundamentals of a Good Fourth-Grade Education*. New York: Doubleday, 1992. Print.

Hirsch, E. D. *What Your Fifth Grader Needs to Know: Fundamentals of a Good Fifth-Grade Education*. New York: Doubleday, 1993. Print.

Hirsch, E. D., and John Holdren. *What Your Kindergartner Needs to Know: Preparing Your Child for a Lifetime of Learning*. New York: Doubleday, 1996. Print.

Hirsch, E. D. *What Your Second Grader Needs to Know: Fundamentals of a Good Second-Grade Education*. Rev. Ed. New York: Dell, 1998. Print.

Hirsch, E. D., and Linda Bevilacqua. *What Your Preschooler Needs to Know*. New York, NY: Bantam Dell, 2008. Print.

"K-12 Curriculum." *Cedarburg*. N.p., n.d. Web. June 2019. http://www.cedarburg.buildyourowncurriculum.com/public/Landing_Grades.aspx.

"Wikepedia.com." *Wikepedia.com*. N.p., n.d. Web. 30 Accessed 2019.

From the author...

I am confident that all parents share in my passion for helping elementary school-age children learn and grow. Together we can empower our kids with the reinforcement of essential knowledge and facts learned in the primary grades. We can strive to provide them the tools to become life-long learners and informed members of our global society, even in their formative years.

If you found value in *Ask Me Smarter*, would you be so kind as to take a minute to write an honest review? Reviews generally consist of: *What the readers learned; how the book affected or benefited their life; and what they would say to someone who was thinking about using this resource as a supplemental teaching tool.*

If you believe that a family with young children might benefit from knowing what to ask and when to ask it with this progressive question and answer format, I respectfully ask you to please direct this family to the grade appropriate *Ask Me Smarter* book on my website for more insight:

www.askmesmarter.com

Finally, please keep in mind that the **Ask Me Smarter** series is available for Preschool and Kindergarten; Grade 1; Grade 2; Grade 3; Grade 4; and Grade 5. All grade levels are also available as an eBook – downloadable to any device!

Your kids await!

Go ahead and *"Ask Them Smarter,"* build their confidence, and empower them with essential knowledge! Because school never closes and learning never ends! Because knowledge is *potential* power!

AMS! – Making knowledge **FUN**-da-men-tal!

CPSIA information can be obtained
at www.ICGtesting.com
Printed in the USA
LVHW080233171120
671909LV00015B/102